REFLECTIONS ON THE FIRST MULTI-PARTY PARLIAMENT, 1995-2000

Pius Msekwa

DAR ES SALAAM UNIVERSITY PRESS LTD.

Published in Tanzania by
Dar es Salaam University Press Ltd.
P.O. Box 35182
Dar es Salaam
Tanzania

ISBN 9976 60 333 9

CONTENTS

PART ONE

CONTRIBUTIONS TO THE CONSTITUTI0NAL DEBATE

PART TWO

EXPOSITIONS ON SOME ASPECTS OF PARLIAMENTARY PROCEDURES UNDER MULTI-PARTYSM

ACKNOWLEDGMENTS

This publication is a result of work done in the preparation of papers for delivery as public lectures to a variety of audiences at different times. I am heavily indebted to all the groups who participated in the discussions of my presentations. Their questions and comments enabled me to alter and improve on some aspects of the original texts.

In a very special way, I want to acknowledge the services of my Office Management Secretary Ms. Esther Bashweka, who, with rare patience diligence and speed, produced all the typescripts from my handwritten drafts.

I also, wish to express my gratitude to all my colleagues and friends for their advice and encouragement; and in particular to Mr. Kileo Nyambele, the Chief Librarian of the Parliament Library, for going carefully through the manuscript and making such corrections as were necessary.

The production of this book would not have been possible without the kind sponsorship of UNESCO (Dar es Salaam office) which provided a generous grant to cover the entire cost of reprinting two thousand copies. This grant has made it possible for the book to be given free of charge to school libraries and to secondary school teachers of Civic Education. I wish to express my grateful thanks to UNESCO (Dar es Salaam office) for this generous support to the worthwhile civic education project in Tanzania.

PREFACE

The first five years of multi-party parliamentary democracy in Tanzania have generally been a period of learning to operate a new political system, and endeavouring to create a new political culture. Because Tanzania was previously under the influence of the one-party political system for more than thirty years, the introduction of multi-party politics on 1st July, 1992, brought with it new experiences which, in some respects, were somewhat alien to a substantial number of people in the relevant age-groups, who had been born and brought up under the mono-party political system. For example, with regard to the institution of parliament, concepts such as "the official opposition," "shadow cabinet," "opposition whips," were entirely new and actually never heard of before. Valid questions were often asked about the functioning of parliament under multi-partyism; about the role of the opposition in parliament, and about the effects of party discipline over its members of parliament, especially those belonging to CCM, the ruling party. Many people also wanted to know the difference between the former one-party parliament and the present multi-party parliament, largely because what they had expected of a multi-party parliament did not quite materialize or measure up to their great expectations of seeing some exciting "fireworks" in the House. Furthermore, there were some heated exchanges of views regarding the need for a new state constitution which will cater for the new multi-party political situation now obtaining in the country.

The essays contained in this collection were written by the author at different times in the course of the last five years. They were aimed at providing answers to some of the questions cited above, as part of the civic education programme which was designed in order to help create a better understanding of the proper fuctioning of a multi-party parliamentary democracy and thereby, hopefully, contribute to the creation of a new political culture which basically provides for the accommodation and tolerance of opposing views and opinions. In this connection, the basic operational culture which we endeavoured to develop inside parliament was that while the majority (CCM) must have their way; the minority (opposition) must also have their say.

This book is intended to serve all those who have an interest in the progress of the democratization process is Tanzania, but it will be especially useful to school teachers and students taking the civics subject.

vii

PART ONE

1

CONSTITUTIONS AND THE CONSTITUTION-MAKING PROCESS IN TANZANIA

INTRODUCTION

I stated in my book entitled *The Transition to Multi-Partyism in Tanzania*, (Dar es Salaam University Press, 1995), that in order for human beings to be able to provide for their material needs more easily, to satisfy their spiritual desires more completely, and to develop their cultural aspirations more richly; they need to associate closely with each other. But once the association is achieved, the resulting community needs to be organised in some definite way, by providing specific leadership organs which will generally coordinate the work of its members and reconcile their conflicting interests. This is true of social clubs, associations, cooperative enterprises, and other registered groups. But when we consider the wider association of people within a nation state, the organs which must be specifically provided for in its constitution are the *Executive*, the *Legislative* and the *Judicial* institutions.

A country's constitution may therefore be defined as that country's basic or fundamental law, which lays down its executive, legislative and judicial institutions. It describes the functions of each of those institutions, and provides for the distribution of powers among them. The present Constitution of the United Republic of Tanzania 1977, fits exactly into the above definition. It has a total of ten chapters. Chapter one declares the fundamental principles of state policy; and the fundamental rights and duties of the country's citizens.

Chapters two through six make provisions for the establishment of the three branches of state authority, namely: the executive, the legislature and the judiciary: and describes the distribution of powers and functions among them.

Chapter seven makes provisions regarding the finances of the United Republic.

Chapter eight establishes the local government authorities of the cities, municipalities and the rural districts.

Chapter nine makes provisions for the existence and control of the Armed Forces of the United Republic.

The last chapter, which is chapter ten, makes essential miscellaneous provisions, such as the procedure for the resignation of persons who hold any of the offices which are established by the Constitution, and also provides definitions for some of the terms which are used in the Constitution.

These are the contents of the Constitution of the United Republic of Tanzania, 1977.

CONSTITUTION MAKING *VS* AMENDING THE CONSTITUTION

Enacting a new constitution of a country or state is a separate and distinct process, from that of amending an existing constitution. The established practice in Tanzania and other Commonwealth African countries, is that a new constitution is enacted by a legislative body generally known as a *Constituent Assembly:* while an existing constitution is amended by Parliament itself, which uses special procedures in carrying out this special legislative function.

Circumstances Which Necessitate the Enactment of a New Constitution

The established practice here in Tanzania and in other Commonwealth countries, is that a new constitution is normally enacted where any of the following events occur:

a) Where there is a change of sovereignty;

b) Where there is a merger of sovereignty;

c) Where the previous constitution was abrogated by a dictatorial regime;

d) Where a new constitution has to be enacted to replace a totally unacceptable one which was put in place by an apartheid regime, when that regime is removed from power by the forces of democracy;

e) Where special circumstances arise, requiring a new constitution to be enacted.

Some Examples of Such Events

a) A change of sovereignty occurred in this country when Tanganyika attained republican status in December 1962: whereby the state's executive power was transferred from the British Monarch who was Head of State of Tanganyika under the previous constitution, to an elected President who now became Head of State. This event necessitated the enactment of new Republican Constitution.

b) A merger of sovereignty occurred in our country in April 1964, when the sovereign Republic of Tanganyika merged with the sovereign Peoples' Republic of Zanzibar to form one sovereign United Republic of Tanzania. That event necessitated the enactment of a new constitution for the new sovereign state.

c) A new constitution was enacted in Uganda in 1995, after its 1962 Independence Constitution was abrogated in 1966 by Milton Obote, the then Prime Minister of Uganda. A process of writing a new constitution was thereby instituted which, on completion, produced the 1967 Uganda Constitution. This Constitution was in turn abrogated in 1971 by Idi Amin Dada who came to power through a military coup. When eventually the National Resistance Movement came to power in 1986, measures were again put in place for the enactment of a new constitution, which is the current Constitution of the Republic of Uganda.

d) When the obnoxious apartheid regime was eventually defeated in South Africa, the process of writing a new democratic constitution was put in place, which eventually produced the 1996 Constitution of the Republic of South Africa.

e) The Nyalali Commission recommended the restructuring of the Union by introducing the federal principle of three governments. Had that recommendation been accepted, that would have created the kind of special circumstances envisaged here, because it would have necessitated the enactment of a new constitution for Tanganyika; as well as a new federal constitution for the United Republic.

The Need for Interim Constitutional Arrangements in the Process of Making a New Constitution

When any of the above mentioned events occur, thus necessitating the enactment of a new constitution, the usual practice is to promulgate an interim constitution which will govern the country during the interim period while the process of enacting a new constitution is taking place. However, in the case of the Republican Constitution of Tanganyika, there was no need to promulgate an interim constitution because the 1961 Independence Constitution was already in place and continued to have effect until it was replaced on 9th December, 1962 by the new Republican Constitution.

But immediately after the Union of Tanganyika and Zanzibar, an interim constitution was adopted, which governed the newly formed United Republic until a permanent constitution came into force in 1977. Similarly, when the National Resistance Movement came to power in Uganda, it proclaimed an interim constitution designated as Legal Notice No. 1 of 1986, which formed the constitutional basis for the governance of Uganda in the interim period until a permanent constitution was enacted. South Africa too, was governed by an interim constitution during the interim period of two years before the enactment of their permanent 1996 Constitution.

The Meaning of "Constituent Assembly"

As has already been stated, the normal practice in Tanzania and other African Commonwealth countries has been that a new constitution is enacted by a legislative body which is designated as a "Constituent Assembly." This unique procedure serves two purposes. First, it is intended to signify the special legal sanctity of the constitution, by giving it a separate procedure entirely distinct from the ordinary legislative procedure which is followed when enacting ordinary laws. Secondly, it removes the requirement of having to obtain the assent of

6   *Reflections on the First Multi-Party Parliament, 1995-2000*

the Head of State, which is applicable to all other laws which are followed when enacted by Parliament. Unlike ordinary laws which must obtain the assent of the head of state, after enactment by the Constituent Assembly, the constitution takes effect without having to be assented to by the head of state.

It is important to underscore the meaning of the term "Constituent Assembly" because some people have mistakenly assumed that this is a body which can be assembled anyhow. They seem to believe that this is the same as the so-called "National Constitutional Conference" of hand - picked or self appointed people which can be convened for the purpose of enacting a new constitution outside parliament (*Kutunga Katiba nje ya Bunge*). And the only reason given for this strategy of avoiding Parliament is that the august House is dominated by CCM members (80%), hence it will only give effect to the wishes of the ruling party and ignore the views of the opposition!

Any attempt to by-pass Parliament would clearly be unconstitutional and a violation of the cherished principle of the rule of law. To disregard the law making powers of parliament for the only reason that it is dominated by CCM members is tantamount to challenging the sovereignty of the people who elected those members in free and fair elections. Parliament is dominated by CCM members because that was the will of the majority of the electorate who voted in the 1995 general elections. Democracy demands that the manifest will of the voters must be respected.

Furthermore, those assumptions and strategies appear to be based on a serious misunderstanding of the proper meaning of the term "constituent assembly." It should be clearly understood that because the constituent assembly is essentially a legislative body:

a) It must be established by law;
b) The law establishing the constituent assembly must delegate legislative powers to it;
c) Its members cannot be hand-picked or self appointed. They must be elected and given that specific mandate by the people themselves.

In practice, there are two ways of instituting a constituent assembly. One way is to arrange for the election of the members of the constituent assembly by universal adult suffrage, in exactly the same way as elections are held for members of the National Assembly. Its sole mandate will be to deliberate on, and enact, a new constitution by a specified majority. This is the method which was adopted by the National Resistance Movement in Uganda, in its constitution making process by a specified majority. Elections to the constituency assembly took place in March 1994, and the assembly first met on 12th May, 1994 under the chairmanship of the Chief Justice, as required by the statute which established it. But it must be remembered that at that material time there was no National Assembly in existence in Uganda.

The alternative method is for the law to make provision for the conversion of the existing National Assembly into a constituency assembly, for the specific purpose of enacting a new constitution. This was the method adopted in Tanzania in 1962 for enacting the Republican Constitution; and was adopted again in 1977 for enacting the Union Constitution. This was also the method adopted in South Africa in 1994, when the newly elected National Assembly and Senate were jointly converted into a Constituent Assembly for the purpose of deliberating on, and enacting, the new Constitution of the Republic of South Africa, 1996.

DO WE NEED A NEW CONSTITUTION?

The above discussion has concentrated on the mechanics for enacting a new constitution. As has already been stated, a new constitution is enacted only when the objective political conditions mentioned above come into existence, thus necessitating the enactment of a new constitution. The crucial question now is do such conditions exist in Tanzania at the present time, which truly necessitate the enactment of a new constitution? My own answer is NO. At this juncture, I must pause briefly to correct a statement which I made at the time of writing my book in 1995 on the Transition to Multi-partysm in Tanzania. I stated then (at p.108), that "the need for a new constitution which will take into account the new multiparty political situation is quite obvious and cannot be disputed." That statement was unduly influenced by my personal experience of CCM constitutions, whereby a new party constitution has been issued every time major constitutional amendments were made therein. However, having made further advances in my comparative study of state constitutions, my better informed opinion now is that the real need is for amendments to be made to the existing Union Constitution; not for a completely new constitution. This is because the political conditions requiring the enactment of a completely new constitution which we mentioned earlier, are not in existence in Tanzania at the moment.

THE LEGAL PROCESS OF ENACTING A NEW CONSTITUTION

I am of course aware that there is a demand which has been made for the enactment of a completely new constitution of the United Republic. There is sufficient authority to support the view that the constitution of a country is both a *political* document as well as a *legal* document. Two procedural issues arise as a result of this:

i) Because it is a political document, its contents must emanate directly from the people of Tanzania themselves. In other words, the people must he consulted and given a genuine opportunity to express their views and opinions regarding the kind of constitution they want. And as I have said elsewhere, the best forum for obtaining the peoples' views are the local government, village and urban ward assemblies, where every adult resident is entitled to attend, and which keeps proper records of its proceedings.

ii) Because it is a legal document, it must be lawfully established, That is why the text of the official oath e.g. the requirement for members of parliament to swear that they will uphold the Constitution of the United Republic *as by law established* (emphasis added).

I have already explained above that there are only two ways of creating a constituent assembly. If the method of converting the existing national assembly into a constituent assembly is not accepted, then the only alternative is to hold fresh general elections for members of the constituent assembly. In which case the legal process of establishing a new constitution will be as follows:

a) Parliament must first enact a law which will make provisions for creating a constituent assembly. The requisite provisions will include the election of members of the constituent assembly; its composition; its legislative powers; the procedure for the conduct of its business; and the financing of its activities.

b) The second stage would be the holding of general elections for the election of members of the constituent assembly by universal adult suffrage.

c) The final stage would be the adoption of a new constitution by the constituent assembly, and its dissolution immediately thereafter.

A constitution cannot possibly be brought into existence by any group of persons not mandated in accordance with the law, such as the so-called "National Conference" of self-appointed or hand picked personalities.

TRANSITION TO MULTI-PARTYISM NOT SUFFICIENT REASON TO REQUIRE A NEW CONSTITUTION

The only reason which is being advanced in the demand for a new constitution is that because Tanzania has changed from the single party political system to multi-partyism, then the country needs a new constitution. But this argument cannot be sustained in the light of available evidence elsewhere. The mere fact of transition from the single party system to multi-partyism does not involve a change of sovereignty, nor does it create any of the other conditions mentioned earlier, which would necessitate the enactment of an entirely new constitution. It should be noted also that the transition to multi-partyism has not taken place in Tanzania alone. Countries like Zambia, Malawi, Kenya, and Zimbabwe also transited to multi-partysm from single party systems during the same historical period, yet none of those countries enacted a totally new constitution as a result only of such transition; and the opposition parties in those countries were not necessarily disadvantaged because of that. In fact, in both Zambia and Malawi, the opposition parties were able to defeat the hitherto ruling parties in elections which were held on the basis of existing constitutions which had been appropriately amended to accommodate multi-partyism.

In the case of Zambia, after President Chiluba had come to power in October 1991, he did appoint, in 1993, a Constitutional Review Commission, which toured the country to gather peoples' views regarding their constitution. The Commission's finding were subsequently used to effect important amendments to the Zambia Constitution. I believe a similar process also took place in Malawi.

It may be worth mentioning here that the Nyalali Commission did indeed recommend the appointment of a constitutional commission by the President, which would travel widely throughout the country to consult the people and collect their views on, and inputs into, our constitutions. But it must be emphasized that the Nyalali Commission had already recommended a three-government structure of the Union which, if accepted, would have necessitated the writing of a completely new constitution for the state of Tanganyika, and a new federal constitution for the restructured Federal Republic. These would have been special circumstances requiring the enactment of new constitution.

Because the restructuring of the Union did not take place, what we need to do now is to identify those areas which merit consideration for the purpose of introducing amendments.

ISSUES REQUIRING CONSIDERATION FOR AMENDMENTS TO THE EXISTING CONSTITUTION

In various workshops and seminars which have been held in the past two years, notably the workshops organised by the Tanganyika Law Society in November 1996 on "Democratization: Constitutional and Legal Changes," and the workshop organised by the Speaker's Office for members of the Parliamentary Legal and Constitutional Affairs Standing Committee in June 1997; certain specific issues have been raised as meriting consideration. Those which were most frequently mentioned are the following:

i) The inclusion of socialist principles in the Constitution;
ii) The enforcement of human rights and the claw-back nature of Article 30 (2):
iii) The executive powers of the President;
iv) The structure of the Union:
v) The composition of the National Assembly;
vi) The electoral system: a mixture of first-past-the post and proportional representation;
vii) The right of recall of Members of Parliament;
viii) The right to challenge Presidential election results;
ix) Democracy at grass-roots level: the autonomy of local governments:
x) The setting up of a Constitutional Human Rights Commission.

I think it reasonable to say that all the above listed matters merit consideration, and should be included in any government white paper for discussion by the people, in order to find out what the majority view will be on each of these important issues. But having so determined the majority view, appropriate amendments can be made to the relevant Articles of the existing constitution; as well as adding new Articles where necessary. It is my contention that such an amending process will adequately achieve the desired objective of having the kind of constitution which is generally acceptable to the majority of the people of Tanzania under multi-partyism, without having to write a completely new constitution.

THE PROCESS OF AMENDING THE EXISTING CONSTITUTION
Written constitutions usually have a specific provision for the procedure of its amendment. In the Union Constitution of Tanzania, this provision is in Article 98 thereof. Other examples are the Constitution of India, whose procedure for its amendment is in Article 368; and the Constitution of Uganda, where the procedure is found in Articles 258 to 262.

Thus, there is no dispute as to how to go about amending the constitution. Under the provisions of article 98 of the Union Constitution, Parliament is empowered to amend the constitution by a two-thirds majority vote at the third reading stage of the amending Bill. However, in certain specified circumstances, the votes of members of parliament from Tanzania Mainland must be taken separately from those of the Zanzibar members; and a two-thirds majority of each group must be achieved. In view of the promised government white paper containing its own proposals for what it considers to be desirable amendments to the Constitution, and its promise to invite the general public to express their views on those proposals, it is to be expected that when the whole process of constitutional interest articulation and aggregation has been completed, a Bill for the thirteenth constitutional amendment will be presented to Parliament and proceeded with in accordance with the provisions of article 98 of the Constitution.

In concluding this discussion, it might be of interest to recount the South African innovation with regard to constitutional review. The South African Parliament has made provisions in its rules of procedure, for an annual review of that country's constitution. A joint committee of the

National Assembly and the National Council of Provinces of that country has been created and given the responsibility of drawing up recommendations for amendments to the Constitution based on the views of the people. The procedure laid down is that before 1st May of every year. the Committee invites the public to make submissions and proposals on the Constitution. These submissions are then processed by the Committee. and the meritorious ones result in draft amendments to the Constitution. which are presented to parliament for the necessary legislative action.

2

THE ELEVENTH CONSTITUTIONAL AMENDMENTS

INTRODUCTION

On 2nd December, 1994, the Parliament of the United Republic of Tanzania, meeting in Dodoma, enacted the eleventh constitutional amendment. This particular legislation has been the subject of intensive discussion and criticism, especially by the Civil United Front (CUF) political party; whose Secretary-General wrote separately to the Speaker of the National Assembly; and to the Registrar of Political Parties, criticising the said constitutional enactment. However it appears that most of this criticism is based on a misunderstanding.

It happens sometimes that when it becomes necessary for a Judge or Magistrate to interpret a given law, he or she makes reference to what is commonly known in judicial language as "the intention of the legislature." That is to say, the Judge or Magistrate concerned attempts to determine what was the intention of the legislature, (Parliament) in enacting that particular piece of legislation. It would appear that most of the criticism regarding the 11th Constitutional Amendment is based on a misunderstanding of the correct intention of Parliament in enacting this important legislation. The purpose of this chapter is to make a modest contribution towards a better understanding of the contents and purpose of the 11th Constitutional Amendment, as part of the general civic education programme.

THE ESSENCE OF THE CRITICISMS

There are three specific areas of the 11th Constitutional amendment which have been criticised. These are:

a) That the powers of the Zanzibar President have been abrogated by the new provision which says that the Zanzibar President shall not at the same time be a Vice-President of the Union, as is the current practice.

b) That the said 11th amendment is a breach of the 1964 Articles of Union, which had stipulated that the President of Zanzibar shall be a Vice-President of the Union.

c) That it was a breach of the Constitution for Parliament to have enacted the said 11th amendment by a two-thirds majority of the whole House, instead of two thirds majority of the Mainland MPs and two thirds majority of the Zanzibar MPs counted separately.

I will now deal with these issues seriatim. The first criticism, namely that the powers of the Zanzibar President have been abrogated, is clearly misplaced, for the following reasons:

a) The powers and authority of the Zanzibar Government as well as the Zanzibar President, are clearly spelled out in sections 102 and 103 of the Constitution of the United Republic of Tanzania. All those who have read the 11th Amendment Bill as passed by Parliament will readily agree that those sections of the Constitution were not affected at all by the said amendment.

They remain as intact as they have always been in the past. The only addition which was made to section 103 (which concerns the powers of the Zanzibar President), is that before assuming the duties of his office, the Zanzibar President "shall make and subscribe, before the Zanzibar Chief Justice, the oath of allegiance to the Constitution of the United Republic of Tanzania." That new oath will of course be in addition to any other oath which is prescribed by the Constitution of Zanzibar for the due execution of the duties of his office. This additional oath is prescribed in section 13 of the 11th Constitutional

Amendment. Can that small addition be honestly described as an abrogation of the powers of the Zanzibar President?

b) Before the advent of the 11ᵗʰ Constitutional Amendment, the Zanzibar President's membership of the Union Cabinet was entirely dependent upon his/her being appointed by the President, to become the Vice-President of the United Republic. In other words, before assuming the office the Zanzibar President was barred from joining the Union Cabinet despite his/her election as President of Zanzibar. The relevant ouster section reads as follows:

> The Vice President who is also the President of Zanzibar shall assume office of Vice-President after the President has assumed office and formed a Cabinet (emphasis added).

As we all know, the practice at the time of elections has normally been that the Zanzibar elections are held about a week or more *before* the Union Presidential and Parliamentary elections are held. Which means that during the interval between the election of the Zanzibar President and the Union Presidential elections, the Zanzibar President *is not* a member of the Union Cabinet, simply because he/she has not yet assumed the office of Vice-President of the Union.

The 11ᵗʰ Constitutional Amendment has wisely corrected that anormally, by giving the Zanzibar President the right to become a member of the Union Cabinet *immediately upon his/her election as Zanzibar President.* Surely, his powers can not be said to have been abrogated because of that?

The second criticism that the 11ᵗʰ Amendment is a breach of the *1964 Articles of Union* is also misplaced, for two reasons: Firstly, it was definitely not (and could not possibly have been) the intention of the founding fathers of the Union, namely Mwalimu Julius Nyerere and Mzee Abeid Aman Karume, that Zanzibar shall forever be restricted to the vice presidency of the Union, with no chance whatsoever of ever assuming the presidency itself. For if that were the case, President Ali Hassan Mwinyi would never have assumed the presidency of the Union in 1985.

Secondly, the 1964 Articles of the Union clearly stated that the office of wo Vice Presidents was an *interim measure* to be implemented only luring the interim period, before the adoption of a permanent constitution. The relevant section of the 1964 Articles of Union states as follows:

During the interim period, the Constitution of the United Republic shall be the Constitution of Tanganyika so modified as to provide for:

a) A separate Legislature and Executive in and for Zanzibar, from time to time constituted in accordance with the existing law of Zanzibar, and having exclusive authority within Zanzibar for matters other than those which are reserved to the Parliament and Executive of the United Republic i.e. having exclusive authority within Zanzibar for non-Union matters.

b) The office of two Vice Presidents, one of whom (being a person normally resident in Zanzibar) shall be the Head of the aforesaid Executive in and for Zanzibar, and shall be the Principal Assistant of the President of the United Republic in the discharge of his executive functions in relation to Zanzibar,

Part (b) of the above quotation clearly shows that the structure of two Vice-Presidents was intended to be an interim measure to remain effective only until the adoption of a permanent constitution. And indeed, when the permanent constitution was finally adopted in 1977, only one Vice President was appointed in the person of Mzee Aboud Jumbe, the then Zanzibar President. In other words, the interim provision of two Vice-Presidents had ceased to exist, with the introduction of the permanent constitution.

At the same time however, the permanent constitution made provision that the President and Vice President must come from different sides of the Union. That is to say, if the President comes from Tanzania Mainland, the Vice President must come from Zanzibar, and vice versa. Hence come 1985, when the then Zanzibar President, Ndugu Ali Hassan Mwinyi, was elected President of the United Republic, had the 1977 constitutional provision of only one Vice President been retained, the Zanzibar President, Dr Salmin Amour, who took over from Ndugu Ali Hassan Mwinyi, would have automatically ceased to be Union Vice President, in order to avoid the situation of having both the President and Vice President coming from the same side of the Union, namely Zanzibar. However, for some obscure reason, the position of two Vice Presidents was created again, and the Zanzibar President now became second Vice President, which was a departure from what had been stipulated in the 1964 Articles of Union, that the Zanzibar President would be the *first Vice-President.*

Therefore if a breach of the Articles of Union can be claimed at all, then it must have occurred way back in 1985; when what had been intended to be a purely temporary provision of two vice presidents in the interim constitution, was now transformed into a permanent feature and incorporated in the permanent constitution! Hence, the correct "Intention of the Legislature' with regard to the 11ᵗʰ Constitutional Amendment, was to go back to the original position adopted by the permanent Constitution in 1977, of having only one Vice-President for the United Republic: with the proviso that both the President and the Vice-President should not come from the same side of the Union. That is precisely the logic of the 11ᵗʰ Constitutional Amendment.

Thirdly, in the light of the new system of political pluralism, it is desirable and prudent that both the President and Vice President should be members of the same political party, in order to facilitate the smooth running of the government. Since in the new environment of electoral competition between political parties, it cannot be guaranteed that the Zanzibar President and the Union President will always come from the same political party, it would be grossly unwise to retain an out-dated constitutional provision which literally forces the Zanzibar President to become the Vice-President of a Union President who comes from a different political party! That is the other logic of the 11ᵗʰ Constitutional Amendment.

The final criticism that it was a breach of the constitution for Parliament to have enacted the 11ᵗʰ constitutional amendment by a two thirds of the whole House, instead of two-thirds counted separately of the Mainland MPs and the Zanzibar MPs; is clearly based on a misunderstanding of the relevant provisions of the Constitution. The relevant section of the Constitution, in this case is Section 98 (1) (a). Under the provisions of that section, there are only eight specified constitutional matters which can only be altered by two-thirds majority of the Mainland MPs and two thirds majority of Zanzibar MPs voting separately. Those specified matters are the following:

i)   The Continuance of the United Republic;
ii) The Continuance of the office of President of the United Republic;
iii) The Executive authority of the United Republic;

iv) The Continuance of the Parliament of the United Republic;
v) The Executive authority of the government of Zanzibar;
vi) The High Court of Zanzibar;
vii) The List of Union matters;
viii) The total number of members of Parliament from Zanzibar.

All other constitutional matters not included in that list can be amended by two-thirds of all the members of Parliament. It should be clearly understood that the 11th Constitutional Amendment does not touch any of the subjects listed above. Hence it was quite proper for the members of parliament to vote as they did; and the constitutional requirement of two-thirds majority of the whole House was duly satisfied. There is no question therefore of parliament having breached the relevant provisions of the Constitution. For record purposes only, it is perhaps worth mentioning here that even if the requirement of two-thirds majority of Mainland MPs and Zanzibar MPs voting separately were to be applied to the case of the 11th Constitutional amendment; that amendment would still have been carried as the actual voting figures indicated: There are 78 Zanzibar MPs in the Union Parliament. 62 voted YES; 3 voted No; 13 were absent. Hence, more than two-thirds of the Zanzibar MPs voted in favour of the 11th Constitutional Amendment.

URGENTLY REQUIRED: A BETTER UNDERSTANDING OF THE 11TH CONSTITUTIONAL AMENDMENT

There is a quotable which says that "information is power." The current debate on the 11th Amendment clearly underscores the urgent need for maintaining a constant flow of information from the national decision-making factory, which is the Parliament; to the consumers of that information, namely the general public. For lack of accurate and relevant information, some people seem to have formed the erroneous impression that the 11th Constitutional Amendment providing for a single Vice-President for the United Republic (who will not at the same time be the President of Zanzibar), has the ulterior motive of introducing a unitary government which would swallow Zanzibar! In parliamentary language, that is an offence which is called "imputing improper motives" and is strictly forbidden by the Standing Rules. But because parliamentary rules do not govern the general public, the best that can be done to allay such fears is to impart correct information, which indeed is the main purpose of this chapter.

As stated by the learned Justices of the Court of Appeal in their judgement of Civil Appeal case No. 31 of 1994,

> It is a well-known rule of interpretation that a law should not be interpreted in a way which leads to absurdity.

It would, I believe, be appropriate to caution here that the 11th Constitutional Amendment should by no means be interpreted in any way which leads to absurdity, as appears to be happening in the on-going discussion of that amendment.

Those who have not read the 11th Amendment itself may not be aware, for example, that in one very significant way, the said amendment has greatly enhanced Zanzibar's influence in the Union Cabinet, in two ways.

Firstly, in the past, the Zanzibar President's membership of the Union Cabinet was entirely dependent on his/her being appointed Vice-President of the Union, which means that without such appointment he/she was disqualified to sit in the Cabinet. In other words, in the past his/her election as Zanzibar President by itself was *not enough* to qualify him/her for membership of the Cabinet. He/she needed in addition to be appointed Vice President in order to qualify him/her for such membership of the Union Cabinet. But the 11th Constitutional Amendment has given the Zanzibar President immediate right to sit in the Union Cabinet by virtue only of his/her position as President of Zanzibar.

In other words, the 11th Constitutional Amendment has given the Zanzibar electorate the recognition it rightly deserves (but which had so far been withheld), namely that the single action by the people of Zanzibar of voting for their President, is enough to make their President a member of the Union Cabinet without qualification in the form of his/her having to be appointed to the office of Vice-President. Can anyone honestly claim that the Zanzibar President's powers have thereby been eroded or abrogated?

Secondly, in the years when the President of the United Republic will come from the Mainland, Zanzibar's influence will now be much greater in the conduct of Union affairs; simply because Zanzibar will have two top leaders sitting in the Union Cabinet, namely the Vice President who comes from Zanzibar, and the President of Zanzibar himself/herself. In order to facilitate a clearer understanding of this particular point, let us take the following example.

Supposing the current President of Zanzibar, Dr Salmin Amour, is elected Union Vice-President. Under the new arrangements, he will have to vacate the Zanzibar Presidency. Supposing further that the current Chief Minister, Dr Omar Ali Juma, is then elected to succeed Dr Salmin Amour as Zanzibar President, then *both* Dr Salmin Amour and Dr Omar Ali Juma will become members of the Union Cabinet. One would think that this is a positive development in favour of Zanzibar, because it will greatly enhance Zanzibar's influence in the Union Cabinet. In the light of that, can anyone honestly claim that Zanzibar has been "swallowed"?

The good or bad fortune of a nation depends on three factors: "its constitution; the way the constitution is made to work; and the respect it inspires." (Georges Bidaults)

3

THE PROSPECTS OF CONSTITUTIONAL LITIGATION IN TANZANIA*[1]

INTRODUCTION

Let me start by thanking you, Hon. Chief Justice, for your kind invitation to me to come and deliver this opening address, which signifies the official opening of this important seminar. You made it clear in your letter that this particular seminar was organized specifically for Judges. That information initially put me in a state of trepidation. But I quickly picked up enough courage to respond in the affirmative. I was greatly assisted in that process by the realization that a Speaker can surely learn something beneficial to his Parliament, through sharing a few thoughts with the top echelons of the Judicial Branch, so conveniently assembled together for the primary purpose of exchanging invaluable expert experiences and professional knowledge on specially selected topics. In particular, I persuaded myself that this will be a great opportunity for the Speaker of Parliament to hear directly from the proverbial "horse's mouth" comments about a popular and exceedingly durable fiction in judicial circles, namely the idea of "discovering the intention of the legislature" in the process of interpreting statutes, when in actual fact, a Parliament such as ours, is not even remotely aware that it is presumed to have a collective legislative intention, which is so highly regarded by the country's superior courts!

---

*[1] Based on a paper prepared for presentation at a seminar for Tanzania Judges.

Let me preface my presentation by associating this function with two very relevant past opinions and recommendations, in order to show that they have luckily not been forgotten. In the first place, there is the strong opinion which was expressed in August 1970, by Hon. Mr Justice P.T. Georges, who was then the Chief Justice of Tanzania. He said the following:

> In a society which is changing as rapidly as the Tanzania society today, lawyers and judges should keep under constant critical examination their basic approach to the process of decision making. If they stand still while the rest of the society moves, the unhappy result may well be that they will have failed to incorporate into the new pattern of progress the idea that the rule of law has a necessary place in any community where the equality of all men and their human dignity are greatly valued. Failure in this important task will be a tragedy for the new society.

I believe that this particular seminar will in part be doing exactly what was intended by Mr Justice Georges, namely, to give a helping hand to those who are engaged in the moulding of the law in our society, in this task of critical self-examination. The second event which quickly comes to mind as a prelude to this seminar, is the report of the Legal Task Force of the Financial and Legal Management Upgrading Project; which was submitted to the government in August 1995. I was privileged to be a member of that Task Force.

Hence if I may briefly speak in that capacity, I must say that it is gratifying indeed to see that at least one particular recommendation which we made in our report regarding the training of judges, is in fact being implemented. In that report the following specific recommendation was made: "The generally accepted principle is that "Judges should train Judges."

We recommended that programmes for the training of Tanzanian judges be drawn up under the supervision of the Chief Justice, with the assistance, whenever appropriate, from outside experts. Two types of programmes were suggested. These are:

i) Induction courses for newly appointed judges. These should be organized for each judge individually. Each programme may last up to three months and involve both a short course in Tanzania or abroad, and a period of understudying another judge.

ii) Opportunities should be sought so that each judge attends at least one seminar or workshop annually. These should be occasions for the judges to discuss issues of common concern, and to hear and discuss presentations by their colleagues or by outside experts.

It is clearly the case that this is one of those training seminars which were envisaged in the recommendations of the Legal Task Force. I am therefore specially delighted to have been invited to officiate at this function.

Hon Chief Justice, after those preliminary remarks, let me now turn to the subject matter of the seminar itself.

A cursory glance through the list of subjects which have been selected for discussion at this seminar shows that the topic of constitutional litigation and interpretation in Tanzania is among the more important ones. I therefore propose to make some observations on that topic. Thereafter, because of the currency at the moment of the topic of corruption resulting from the publication of the Warioba Report, I propose also to touch briefly on the important question of the independence of the judiciary in relation to the threat of corruption. But another subject on which it would be of great interest to share ideas and experiences is with regard to election petitions. As is well known, there was a flood of election petitions immediately after the 1995 multi-party general election, thus imposing an unexpected and extra heavy burden on the High Court and Court of Appeal. The crucial question which is being raised now is how to control this spate of election petitions, without at the same time interfering with the constitutional right of the individual to have free access to the courts in order to seek redress for his/her grievances. I will not make any comments on this topic myself, but it may well be a useful one for discussion at this seminar.

CONSTITUTIONAL LITIGATION

The preface to the Irish Constitution, which I have had an opportunity to read, contains a statement which says that "the last thirteen years have seen an explosion of constitutional litigation." That preface was written in 1993, hence it is referring to the period of Irish history beginning from 1980. Here in Tanzania, for more than thirty years since independence, there was virtually no constitutional litigation. But I would venture to predict that the next few years may well see an explosion of constitutional litigation in this country, pretty similar to the Irish experience.

EXPECTATIONS OF INCREASED CONSTITUTIONAL LITIGATION IN TANZANIA

I believe that the writing is already on the wall. Because since the enactment in 1992 of Constitutional amendments to make provision for the re-introduction of a multi-party democracy in Tanzania, a number of Tanzanians have already, (if I may borrow Mr Justice Samatta's phraseology in one of his judgements delivered in the High Court sitting at Mtwara) knocked at "the doors of the temple of justice" in order to seek redress for injury which they believe has been caused to them by violating some provisions of the Constitution of the United Republic. But it appears that even more litigation is to be expected, because there are already several pointers in that direction.

For example, in February 1990, Professor Issa Shivji published in book form, his inaugural lecture which he had previously delivered at the University of Dar es Salaam. His book is titled "The Legal Foundations of the Union of Tanzania's Union and Zanzibar Constitutions." In that book, he vigorously challenges the powers of the Union Parliament to amend the list of Union matters as being "unlawful and invalid," and proceeds to issue a warning that "the amending acts could have been inpugned in the domestic courts of Tanzania on ground of repugnancy." He submitted that "these are justifiable issues, and private parties can raise them."

Furthermore, the learned professor makes what appears to me to be a rather strange assertion, that "the 1977 Constitution is subordinate to the 1964 Acts of Union." Was this indeed the intentions of the Constituent Assembly which enacted the 1977 Union Constitution?

Hence if the predicted explosion of constitutional litigation does in fact take place, then these challenges and assertions by Prof. Shivji may well surface and knock at the doors of the temple of justice. Since a seminar of this kind provides an excellent opportunity for the top brass of the Judiciary in Tanzania to widen their knowledge and share experiences from different jurisdictions in handling similar problems, your lordships may want to use the instant opportunity to exchange views on these matters.

THE POTENTIAL FOR CONSTITUTIONAL LITIGATION

But that is not all. There appears to be further potential for increased activities in this area of constitutional litigation in the coming years. In the first place, there are several conspicuous ambiguities in the Kiswahili words which are used in various provisions of the Union Constitution. This makes it possible that your lordships might be called upon, by way of Constitutional litigation, to apply your learned minds to the task of discovering what the intention of the legislature was in enacting the relevant provisions.

Let me cite a few examples of these ambiguities. I will confine my examples only to chapter three of the Constitution which deals specifically with the legislature. This is because in my capacity as Speaker, that is precisely my constitutionally demarcated functional area of responsibility. Take, for example, Article 41(7); which reads as follows:

> Where a candidate is declared by the Electoral Commission to have been elected President, no court shall have jurisdiction to inquire into the matter of his election.

On the fact of it, it would appear that only the Courts are denied jurisdiction to inquire into the matter which is specified in that Article. However, on a close scrutiny of this provisions, it is not clear whether, apart from the Courts, other constitutional organs, such as parliament or a committee thereof, would have jurisdiction to make such an inquiry? In my opinion, this provision is unclear. The position is however stated more clearly in Article 83(2); which states that:

> Where the Electoral Commission ... Has declared a member of Parliament to have been elected President, no court or any other authority shall have jurisdiction to inquire into the question whether or not the seat of that member has become vacant. (emphasis added).

One is tempted to ask: why the difference between these two provisions?

A second example of conspicuous ambiguity is to be found in Article 67(2) of the Constitution, which makes provision for the disqualification of any person from being a member of parliament. The relevant provision reads as follows:

> Where that person has been convicted by any Court in the United Republic, and sentenced to death or to imprisonment for a period exceeding six months on account of any offence, however designated, which arises from a violation of trustworthiness. (emphasis added).

The phrase "violation of trustworthiness" ("Utovu wa uaminifu") is not defined. What then is the kind of offence which would constitute a "violation of trustworthiness?" This clearly requires clarification.

Another example is in Article 90(2), which makes provision for the specified circumstances under which the President may dissolve Parliament before the expiry of its normal term of five years. It reads as follows:

> Where Parliament refuses to enact a law in the circumstances prescribed in article 97(4).

But in article 97(4) there is no mention of parliament refusing to enact a law. Contrary to that, article 97(4) makes provision for a Bill which has been returned to Parliament by the President, and is adopted again by a two-thirds majority. Hence, there is no question here of "Parliament refusing to enact a law." This too requires clarification.

Yet another very conspicuous ambiguity is in Article 71(1)(g); whereby it is stated that unless he sooner dies or resigns, or becomes otherwise disqualified. A Member of Parliament shall continue to hold office as such member until the time of the next general elections.

The phrase "the time of elections" is very vague, because it refers to a period of time, and not a specific day. In other words, the actual cut-off point is not specified. But fortunately this particular matter has now been resolved by the judgement of the Court of Appeal of Tanzania, in Civil Appeal No. 57 of 1997, when, in interpreting that provision, the Court of Appeal declared thus:

We are satisfied that a Member of Parliament under normal circumstances holds office as such a Member until Parliament is dissolved to allow for new general elections to be held.

However, in my opinion, that decision leaves one important issue still unresolved: namely the conflict which then arises between that binding decision, and Article 55(1)(4) of the Constitution, which is a specific requirement that "*All Ministers and Deputy Ministers shall be appointed from among the Members of Parliament.*" So if members of Parliament do cease to be such members upon the dissolution of Parliament, how will that be compatible with article 57(2)(f), which permits ministers (who only qualify to be ministers if they are Members of Parliament) to remain in office even after Parliament is dissolved, and actually beyond election day itself, right up to the time immediately before the President elect takes the oath of office? It appears to me that someone might want to challenge whether a person has powers to carry out ministerial functions after Parliament is dissolved and has thus ceased to be a Member of Parliament.

This point conveniently brings me to the exciting concept of the Courts having to discover "the intention of parliament." In an English Court of Appeal judgement delivered in London on 3rd February, 1995, the British Home Secretary won the right to detain illegal immigrants who are seeking asylum while their applications were being considered. This judgement overturned an earlier ruling by the High Court, which had decided that the Home Office must free anyone seeking asylum while their applications are being considered. Presenting the Court of Appeal judgement, Lord Justice Leggart said the following:

> Parliament cannot sensibly have intended that any illegal immigrant who is apprehended can, by claiming asylum, avoid detention, unless and until his asylum is investigated and dismissed. (emphasis added)

I am warmly enthused by the words that "Parliament could not sensibly have intended" that particular outcome. Let me now borrow those words in asking the following questions: Could our own Parliament sensibly have intended that the two provisions in Article 90(2), and article 97(4), should be so obviously in conflict with each other? Or, could our

Parliament have sensibly intended that the jurisdiction for inquiry should be denied only to the Courts in Article 41(1); but extend that denial to "any other authority" in Article 83(2)? Furthermore, could our Parliament sensibly have intended to introduce the conspicuous ambiguities in the constitution which we have pointed out above? Finally, could our parliament in its collective wisdom, sensibly have intended to create the embarrassing confusion which is embedded in Article 90(2), when read together with Article 97(4)?

I have cited these few examples merely to illustrate the potentially great challenge which faces the Courts in this country; all the more so as more and more people become aware of their constitutional rights which are enforceable through constitutional litigation. It is therefore hoped that through such litigation, the intention of the legislature underlying those provisions will be truly discovered.

OTHER POTENTIAL ATTRACTIONS FOR CONSTITUTIONAL LITIGATION

There are several other potential areas that might attract litigation. I have two examples in mind. The first is to be found in article 71(1)(d); which provides one of the reasons for the unseating of a Member of Parliament. It states as follows:

> Where it is proved that he has violated the provisions of the Public Leadership Code of Ethics.

Section 15 of the Public Leadership Code of Ethics Act, 1995, sates that:

> A public leader who is subject to section 9 shall be considered to have breached the code if:
>
> a) he fails, without reasonable cause, to make a declaration required by that section.

Considering the fact that election petitions are instituted for the same purpose of trying to unseat a Member of Parliament, article 71(1)9d) could be used as yet another convenient opportunity for trying to unseat members of parliament who fall under that provision. This is because section 9 of the relevant Act, requires every Member of Parliament to submit his annual property declaration form to the Speaker, at the end of each year. But in the three years which have elapsed since that law came into force, a number of MPs have routinely failed to meet the deadline, thus violating the relevant provisions. It may well be that they have so far been able to escape punishment only because no procedure has yet been laid down for taking them to Court. When such procedure becomes available, I believe the desire to unseat the violators of that law could lead to litigations on a scale pretty similar to that of the election petitions.

The second potential can be readily discerned from the current constitutional debate. Serious questions have been raised regarding the validity of including one political party's ideological principle, namely *Ujamaa*, in the preamble to a multi-party constitution. I understand that the preamble to the Irish Constitution has been the subject of interpretation by the Irish Courts, where it has been held that the preamble might, on occasion, give rise to binding constitutional norms. There is potential therefore for litigation to be instituted in respect of the *Ujamaa* provision which appears in the preamble to the Constitution of the United Republic. Potentially, situations may arise, for example, whereby people who, having failed to win a competitive tender, will want to bring action claiming that they have been discriminated against merely because they belong to a political party which opposes *Ujamaa*!

One other point which is also being raised in the current constitutional debate and appears to be relevant as a potential for constitution litigation, is in relation to Articles 5(1) and 67(1)(b). The contention is that whereas Article 5(1) states that "Every citizen who has attained the age of 18 years is entitled to vote at an election," thus permitting individuals to elect their leaders, Article 67(1)(b) disqualifies individuals from being elected as private candidates. They have to belong to a registered political party and be sponsored by their party in order to be recognised as candidates for election. Article 67)1)(b) is therefore regarded as unfairly denying un-sponsored candidates their constitutional right of being elected.

This is yet another area where your lordships may, in the course of this seminar, wish to exchange views in an effort to find out what was the intention of the legislature in enacting this particular provision.

THE INDEPENDENCE OF THE JUDICIARY

Let me now say a few words about the all important subject of the independence of the judiciary and the looming serious danger of its being threatened by certain corrupt elements in our society.

Much has of course been said and written about the independence of the judiciary and the question of improper influences affecting the outcome of matters which are for the time being before the Courts. The most popular notion of the independence of the judiciary has normally been that the judiciary should be free from interference by the executive branch of government.

But as a matter of fact, independence of the judiciary means much more than freedom from interference by the executive, or by the legislature. Article 2 of the General Assembly Resolution 146, in stating the basic principles regarding the independence of the Judiciary, stipulates as follows:

> The Judiciary shall decide matters before it impartially, on the basis of facts and in accordance with the law, without any restrictions, improper influences, inducements, pressures, threats of interference, direct or indirect, from any quarter or for any reason.

The reference in this definition to "improper influence and inducements from any quarter" is clearly inclusive of sources other than the executive and the legislature. Corruption is undoubtedly a major source which constitutes a far more serious compromise on the independence of the Judiciary, and is greatly damaging to the community as a whole. I would therefore suggest that this seminar should allocate some time for a serious discussion of this cancer of corruption in the Judiciary, and how it can be cured. This will be a positive response to the numerous public complaints which have been made against corruption in the Judiciary, as reported by the Warioba Commission.

Before I leave the topic of interference in the affairs of the Judiciary, let me ask one relevant question. In 1964 the British House of Lords in its judicial capacity, considered the question whether the British Government had a duty at common law to pay compensation to a British oil company whose installations in Burma had been destroyed by British forces during the second world war, in order to save the property from falling to the Japanese army. The destruction of the installations had been carried out on the orders of the Crown, in the lawful exercise of its prerogative power to provide for the defence of the British Territory. It was held that there was no common law right to compensation for damage inflicted by the Crown's forces while actually fighting the enemy; but that destruction of property for the purpose of denying its use to the enemy did give rise to such a right. The oil company was consequently awarded compensation.

However, that decision was immediately nullified by the enactment of the War Damages Act of 1965, which prevented the payment of compensation in that, or any similar case. Here in Tanzania, we have on record the case of Mangi Mkuu Thomas Marealle who, upon the enactment of the abolition of the Chiefs Ordinance in 1963, went to court to claim compensation from the Chagga District Council for loss of office. He succeeded and was awarded a princely sum of Stg. Pounds 45,000/=. The National Assembly quickly nullified the court decision through appropriate legislation. My question is: Can these events be looked upon as interference by the legislature in the affairs of the judiciary? I stand to be corrected, but my own personal view is that in the absence of an internally generated self correction initiative by the courts themselves, a positive intervention like this by the executive or the legislature in an effort to remedy some specific shortcomings, could facilitate better administration of justice. Hence this kind of positive intervention should not at all be regarded as interference with the independence of the Judiciary. As Isabella says in Shakespeare's *Measure for Measure*:

> O, it is excellent, to have a giant's strength,
> But it is tyrannous, to use it like a giant.

In their separate jurisdictions both the legislature and the judiciary can be rated as having the strength of a giant. But, as advised by Shakespeare, it would be tyranny for any of them to use that strength like a giant.

CONCLUSION

I have now come very close to the end of my presentation. Let me therefore conclude with a plea. In this presentation, I have made reference to the well-known doctrine of the independence of the judiciary. I think I should also draw attention to the twin doctrine which is equally well-know, that of the supremacy of parliament.

The relationship between the judiciary and parliament in Tanzania has fortunately always been cordial. So far so good. But, as the Makerere University motto says, we have to build for the future: *pro futuro edificamus*. My plea here is that in order to ensure that in future each of these two branches of government, namely the judiciary and the legislature, clearly knows its powers and limitations in relation to the other, very clear constitutional provisions should be made soon to that effect. Under our Constitution, the judiciary is empowered to perform various checking functions on the legislature. These include Judicial review and interpretation of the Constitution. At the same time, the principle of the supremacy of parliament underscores the fact that it can make and unmake any law in our land. This could be interpreted to mean that whatever is done lawfully by Parliament cannot be undone by any other body or person. I submit therefore that there is an urgent need for a clearer distinction to be made between the roles of these two important organs of state, in order to establish the necessary comity between them, while at the same time maintaining the established principle of checks and balances.

The Irish experience shows that in a number of cases, the most recent being the 1987 Supreme Court Judgement in Crotty vs An Taoiseach (1987) IR 713: the Irish courts have sought to identify the limits of judicial power with a view to preventing judicial encroachment on the legislative functions: while the legislative process itself has been identified as being beyond the scope of judicial review, other than in accordance with Article 26 of the Irish Constitution, which confers on the Supreme Court the duty, upon the reference to it of a bill passed by both Houses of Parliament for decision whether such bill or any specified provision thereof, is repugnant to the Constitution. I submit that we do need something of that kind reflected also in our constitution.

Finally, Hon Chief Justice, I would like to conclude with a light touch, by quoting an obscure 16th century proverb, which reads as follows:

Few physicians live well.
Few lawyers die well.

I presume that the proclamation "few lawyers die well" is still in force. So, be prepared!

Hon. Chief Justice, It is now my very pleasant duty to declare this continuing Legal Education Training Seminar for Judges, officially open.

Thank you.

4

THE CHALLENGE OF MULTI-PARTY ELECTORAL ORGANIZATION: THE TANZANIAN EXPERIENCE

INTRODUCTION

This chapter discusses the organisation and conduct of multi-party elections using Tanzania as a case study. Tanzania formally adopted the multi-party political system with effect from 1st July, 1992; when the country's constitution was amended in order to cater for that new system. However, elections were not held immediately thereafter, because it was prudently felt that the democratisation process must be properly planned, in order to achieve a smooth and orderly transition from the one party system of government which had been in place in Tanzania for nearly three decades, to the new multi-party system. In particular, it was agreed that the newly formed political parties must be given sufficient time to establish and consolidate themselves; to recruit their members, and to design and propagate their policies country wide. Hence it was decided to allow the existing parliament which had been elected in October, 1990, to complete its full five-year term up to October, 1995, when the first multi-party parliamentary elections would be held. As programmed, these elections were successfully held on 29th October, 1995. What then is Tanzania's overall experience with regard to the challenge of multi-party electoral organisation?

ELECTORAL ORGANISATION

The basic challenge of electoral organisation focuses mostly on the following three agencies, namely:

a) the government:

b) the Electoral Authority;

c) the political parties.

Parliamentarians are only the product of the electoral process. Thus they play no major part in the process itself.

THE ROLE OF THE GOVERNMENT AND THE ELECTORAL AUTHORITY

The primary responsibility of the government as far as elections are concerned is the enactment of an appropriate elections law which will provide a level playing field for all the participating political parties and candidates: plus the appointment of an impartial electoral authority which will administer the whole election process. In the case of Tanzania, these functions were carried out without any difficulty because an Elections Act was already in existence. Even under the one party system of government, the elections law had been designed so as to afford "a fair and equal opportunity" to the competing candidates. All that was required, therefore, was to recast the existing law so as to afford the same "fair and equal opportunity" to the competing political parties under the new multi-party system.

Similarly, a new high-powered Electoral Commission was appointed well in advance of the election date, and given the necessary mandate to plan and prepare for the elections. Acute problems arose, however, with regard to providing the Electoral Commission with adequate funds and other facilities which were necessary and sufficient for the efficient management of the election exercise. Tanzania has no permanent register of voters, the registration of voters has to be carried out each time there is a general election or even a by-election. This is always an expensive exercise. But it became even more expensive this time because, as a result of a low turn-out, the one month registration period had to be extended by an additional ten days which had previously not been budgeted for. But the greatest impact of late funding and general maladministration by the Electoral Commission was felt on election day itself. For example, many incidences were reported of late arrival of election materials at polling stations: lack of transport for election officials etc. But fortunately these problems were not of such a nature as to affect significantly the results of the election, except for the capital city of Dar es Salaam, where the administrative problems were so serious that the Electoral Commission was obliged to cancel the polling exercise. Polling in Dar es Salaam took place three weeks later, on 19th November, 1995.

The opposition parties repeatedly said that they had no confidence in the Electoral Commission, which they accused of being biased in favour of the ruling party. However, such criticism was largely unfair because it was based on mere suspicion that because the Commission had been appointed by the government, it would be tempted to favour the governing party. This was unfair because the Electoral Commission members were high judicial officers who should be trusted to carry out their duties without fear or favour. But the criticism seems to have affected the Commission. Presumably in order to prove that they were impartial, they initially discarded the long established practice of appointing election officials from among the civil servants, and started inviting applications from unemployed people for the important positions of Returning Officers and Presiding Officers. This created immense problems of accountability and administrative failures, due to lack of experience in election administration.

The role of government is indeed of supreme importance. A report which was published in the *Nairobi Daily Nation* newspaper of Tuesday, March, 12th 1996, had the following observation:

> The US which is keenly watching a number of African States as they go through their second round of multi-party elections has identified four common constraints to free and fair elections in a number of countries, according to a top State Department Official. Among the constraints are denying opposition parties access to government controlled mass media; a lack of freedom of assembly; ruling parties instituting laws at the last minute to exclude the opposition candidates; and opposition parties suffering from a lack of resources.

Tanzania's general election of October, 1995 was the country's first round of multi-party elections. But it already shows clearly that serious efforts were made by the government to overcome the above listed constraints, as shown below.

i) The Issue of Denying Opposition Parties Access to Government Controlled Mass Media

This constraint was removed by amending section 53 of the Elections Act in the following manners:

53 1) Subject to subsection (2), the candidate for the office of the President and Vice-President of the United Republic, and the political parties participating in an election, shall have the right to use the state radio and television broadcasting service during the official period of the election campaign.

2) The Electoral Commission shall, after consultation with the candidates and political parties concerned, and the officers responsible for the public media, coordinate the use of the broadcasting rights under this section.

3) Every print media owned by the government which publishes any information relating to the electoral process, shall be guided by the principle of total impartiality, and shall refrain from any discrimination in relation to any candidate both in the manner they treat the candidates journalistically and in the amount of space dedicated to them.

4) For the purpose of giving effect to this section, the Commission may issue binding directives to any government owned media."

These amendments were enacted by the Parliament of the United Republic of Tanzania on 21st April, 1995, well before the official campaign period, which started on the date when Parliament was dissolved, namely August 4th, 1995.

These new provisions were carefully observed by all the government controlled mass media, as evidenced by the fact that no complaints were registered in that area.

ii) The Issue of Lack of Freedom of Assembly

This constraint was also removed by legislation, through an amendment Act which removed the necessity for candidates or their political parties to seek permission to obtain permits from government officials or the police in order to hold public campaign meetings. The amended provision reads as follows:

(5)1) Where there is a contested election in constituency, the election campaign shall be organised by the candidate, the candidate's political party or by his agent.

2) The candidate, his agent or the candidate's political party, as the case may be, shall supply the Returning Officer with a schedule indicating the proposed programme for the public meetings of the candidate's campaign specifying the time and places of those meetings.

3) A Returning Officer may call a meeting of all the candidates or their agents for the purpose of coordinating the campaign programme of the candidates.

4) Every Returning Officer shall cause a copy of the coordinated programme to be submitted to the District Commissioner and the police officer commanding within the constituency, and such programme shall constitute a notice of the proposed meetings for the purposes of the Police Ordinance.

iii) The Issue of Ruling Parties Instituting Laws to Exclude Opposition Candidates

This did not happen with regard to the Tanzania general elections of October, 1995. On the contrary, the Elections Act contains penal provisions for any one who might try to discourage any person from standing as a candidate. The relevant provision reads as follows:

(89) 1) Any person holding any official office or acting in any official capacity who, in the exercise of the functions of such office or in such official capacity, makes any statement or does any act with intent to discourage any other person from seeking nomination under this act, or to procure any person who has been nominated to withdraw his candidature, shall be guilty of an offence and shall, on conviction, be liable to a fine not exceeding ten thousand shilling or to imprisonment for a term not exceeding twelve months, or to both such fine and imprisonment.

iv) The Issue of Lack of Resources on the Part of the Opposition

This constraint was removed by the government's decision to grant an election expenses subsidy in the sum of one million shillings per candidate irrespective of parties. Therefore all the competing candidates had the same amount of money in every constituency.

These were no doubt very crucial decisions which were taken by the Tanzania government in order to provide a free and fair playing field for all the participating parties and candidates.

THE ROLE OF POLITICAL PARTIES IN ELECTIONS

One of the basic functions of political parties is to provide a suitable forum for the participation of individual citizens in political socialization, because they are the only social structures which are capable of involving large numbers of people in political action on a sustained and controlled basis. Unless the particular interests of an individual are at stake, that individual does not have to engage in extensive and continuos articulation of his general interests. His political party assures him that his general interests will be safeguarded with minimal personal involvement on his part. Hence the absolute centrality of political parties in the organisation and conduct of elections.

The Tanzanian Experience

In the Tanzanian context. political parties have been defined by the Political Parties Act (No. 5 of 1992) as follows:

> Political Party means any organised group which is formed for the purpose of forming a government or a local Authority within the United Republic through elections: or for putting up or supporting candidates to such elections.

Therefore, in the context of that definition. the primary purpose. or indeed the *raison d'etre* of a political party in Tanzania. is to participate in elections with a view to acquiring power. at both the local government level and the national level. Any group which does not have these clearly stated aims and objectives does not qualify to be registered as a political party. Such group can only be permitted to operate legally if it is registered under a different law. which provides for the registration of civil societies. That law is known as The Societies Ordinance. (Cap. 337 of the Laws of Tanzania). Political scientists have identified three major roles for political parties in relation to an election. all of which are of equal importance in winning the election. These are:

a) Candidate selection:

b) Organisation and management of the election campaign;
c) Voter identification and targeting.

Candidate Selection

The selection of candidates is, of course, the first crucial step. Twelve political parties decided to participate in Tanzania's first multi-party elections, in order to compete with the only hitherto ruling party, making a grand total of thirteen parties. Candidate selection within the ruling party turned out to be a complex undertaking. All the out-going MPs, without exception, were members of that party, careful consideration had to be given to the question whether, for each parliamentary seat, the incumbent should be re-selected or whether a new comer should be selected instead. In order to resolve this particular question, the ruling party introduced new procedures for primary nomination and final nomination of its candidates. According to these new procedures, any interested member of the party was free to apply for nomination in a constituency of his choice.

The first stage was for all the applicants to go through a primary process of selection, whereby a series of meetings of party delegates within the constituency were asked to cast their preference votes for the applicants. The preference votes for all the applicants were then submitted to the Party headquarters for the final selection of one candidate for each constituency by the party's national executive committee. Although the vast majority of the incumbents were finally selected, the number of casualties was quite considerable. The most important determining factor in this case seems to have been the incumbent applicant's previous performance. But the scourge of corruption is also reported to have influenced the primary selection process in some cases.

Fortunately however, the issues of tribalism and religion which normally tend to accompany elections in many other countries, had no significant influence at any stage in the selection process in Tanzania.

With only slight variations, a similar process of primary nominations was followed by all the opposition parties. An interesting, and perhaps strikingly unique feature of candidate selection in Tanzania was the emergency of a significant number of what might be described as "frivolous candidates." A frivolous candidate is a person who clearly has no chance whatsoever of winning a given election, but who nonetheless presents himself as a candidate for that election. The invitation to frivolous candidates was probably unintended and unplanned. It emanated from a decision by the government, to pay a subsidy to each political party in the sum of one million Tanzania Shillings (approximately USD 2,000) for every constituency candidate supported by any party. This turned out to be a very attractive income generation activity for all the political parties. Hence some of the small parties went out of their way to persuade people to stand as candidates in order to enable those parties to qualify for the government subsidy.

This was a unique development because the principal objective of any political party should be to select a candidate who is most likely going to win the election. and not just any candidate!

Organisation and Management of the Election Campaign

After the parties had selected their candidates, the second step was the organisation and management of the election campaign. The primary purpose of an election campaign is to communicate a message which will convince a majority of the electorate. Hence, it is the responsibility of each party to set out themes or issues which the electorate will find more convincing than those of its opponents.

The ideal model of contested elections between political parties assumes that each party will put forward a set of detailed issue position, which will give the voters very clear alternatives to choose from. This ideal model also assumes that the voters fully understand the alternatives which are being offered to them, and that they will rationally, make their choices on the basis of that understanding.

However. the Tanzania experience of the 1995 general election shows that these assumptions do not always hold true. For example, in the circumstances of Tanzania, where more of the issues are "bread and butter" issues which must necessarily focus on the need to enhance the social and economic development of the people, the majority of the voters would not be able to correctly identify the difference in the positions or policies of the different parties.

In these circumstances, the focus of the campaign was more on the personal qualities of the competing candidates. That is to say, the majority of voters tended to assess the candidates individually in order to see which one of them had the desired leadership qualities of ability, integrity and trustworthiness.

In other words, while in theory the electorate was asked to make a choice between competing political parties; but in practice, except in a few specific cases, the choice was influenced more by the qualities of the individual candidates, irrespective of his or her political affiliation. Therefore the election campaign became, in essence, entirely candidate oriented, instead of being party oriented, which is probably a good thing, because it will encourage political parties to select people with the right leadership qualities as their election candidate.

Voter Identification and Targeting

A political party's third and final step is the mobilisation of votes. This is known as the get-the-votes strategy whose purpose is to bring as many as possible of the party's supporters to the polls on election day so that they may vote for the party's candidates.

This is the area where the competing political parties in Tanzania showed the greatest weakness and inexperience. Voter targeting is not an easy task, because there are usually three different categories of voters to deal with. The first category consists of those who support the party strongly; the second category consists of those who oppose it strongly; and the third category is that of the undecided voters or whose preferences are not so rigid and can be changed by the impact of the election campaign. The political parties in Tanzania have not yet developed an appropriate strategy for handling this crucial function of voter-targeting.

An experienced political party would work very hard to identify and fully mobilise the first category of "strong supporters," as well as the third category of the "undecided" voters, by persuading them to vote for the party's candidate. In the Tanzania general elections of October, 1995, this did not happen.

The ruling party wrongly assumed that the opposition parties were weak and immature, and grossly over estimated its own support, which it mistakenly believed was very strong throughout the country. The ruling party therefore made no special effort to target the voters.

On their part, the opposition parties also wrongly assumed that the ruling party was hopelessly unpopular and would therefore be easily thrown out of office. Hence the opposition parties tended to concentrate on trumpeting the presumed failures of the ruling party and hoped that that would be enough for them to win the election.

Political parties in the new multi-party democracies in Africa still have a long way to go in terms of learning and applying the appropriate campaign strategies. For example, apart from the voter categories of strong supporters and strong opponents, there is also another category of electors who have to be handled in mobilising votes. This is the category of abstainers. Unfortunately, it is too often taken for granted that all the people who are entitled to vote will in fact do so on polling day, except only those who might be prevented from going to the polls by reasons which are beyond their control, such as sickness or essential travel outside the constituency. Experience, however, has shown that in every single election there are far more abstentions than can be attributed to reasons beyond their control. In fact, there are two broad groups of abstainers. The first group is that of the "positive" abstainers, the other group is that of the "negative" abstainers. The positive or active abstainers are those who deliberately decide not to vote just because the candidates do not appeal to them or even as a form of protest where, for example, followers of a certain minority party have no candidate of their party standing for election in that particular constituency. These might well be persuaded by their consciences to join the abstantion camp. The "negative" abstainers, on the other hand, are those who are generally not interested in politics, the kind of people who either never vote anyway, or happen to vote only if it does not entail the slightest personal botheration to them. As part of a political party's overall get-the-votes strategy, these two groups of potentially non-voting people have some how got to be persuaded to change their habits.

There also exist special voter-targeting techniques of "broadcasting" and "narrow-casting" when sending out campaign messages to votes. "Broadcasting" means the art of beaming specialised messages to specific voter groups. Probably because of lack of appropriate experience, the political parties in Tanzania did not make use of these campaign techniques.

THE ROLE OF ELECTION OBSERVERS

Because of the need to ensure that elections are free and fair, it has now become standard practice for a country which is holding elections to invite groups of observers to monitor the elections. The primary role of election monitoring is to ensure fairness and equality of opportunity between the participating parties. Tanzania has a very long experience of election monitoring.

Right from the time when the constitutional one-party system was introduced in Tanzania in1965, great care was taken to make legislative provision for the appointment of "supervisory delegates," whose function was to oversee every step in the election process, from the nomination of candidates to the actual voting and counting of votes. These delegates had to be persons who are not residents of the district to which they were assigned. Their specific mandate was to ensure that each candidate was given a "far and equal opportunity" throughout the election process. These arrangements worked very well for all the elections which were held every five years from 1965 until 1990. However, with the introduction of the mult-party political system in July, 1992 the provisions for the appointment of supervisory delegates were deleted from the Elections Law.

The practice now is to allow groups of observers, both foreign and local, to witness the proceedings in order to be able to say whether or not, in their objective opinion, the relevant elections were free and fair. The presence of election observers does indeed add credibility to the results of the election. But for a vast country like Tanzania, there were not enough election observers to go to every place in order to keep an eye on what was happening. Furthermore, election observers tend to concentrate on the activities of election day alone, whereas the election process actually begins with the registration of voters, through the election day itself. Any malpractices which may have been committed during any of those stages will have escaped the attention of the observer groups.

CONCLUSION

In multi-party elections, the Challenge of electoral organisation is clearly a shared responsibility between the government and its electoral authority on the one hand; and the participating political parties and their candidates on the other. In the light of Tanzania's experiences of the 1995 first multi-party general election, all the major actors on the election stage still have a long way to go.

The government and its electoral authority certainly need to greatly improve their performance in the planning and administration of elections; and the political parties need to improve on their campaign management strategies. With regard to election observers, while it is accepted that they have an important role to play in giving credibility to the results of an election, they are hopelessly disadvantaged if their observation is limited to voting day. Hence any malpractices which may have been committed during the earlier stages of the election process will have escaped their attention. Their usefulness could be greatly enhanced by having them in place right from the beginning of the electoral process.

5

THE WHITE PAPER APPROACH TO DISCUSSING
AMENDMENTS TO THE CONSTITUTION

INTRODUCTION

The *Oxford Advanced Learner's Dictionary* defines the word "White paper" as follows:

> A report published by the government about its policy on a matter that is to be considered by Parliament.

This is originally a conventional British parliamentary procedure which has been adopted by several countries which were once British colonies or British administered territories. Tanzania belongs to this group of countries, hence on attaining independence in 1961, the procedure of government white papers was adopted in this country.

The first ever government white paper to be introduced after independence was Government Paper No. 1 of 1962, which was entitled "Proposals of the Tanganyika Government for a Republic." On that occasion, the government was making proposals for a new Republican Constitution of Tanganyika. These proposals were set out clearly and extensively in that paper, using simple non-legal language, in order to make them meaningful to the general public. The paper containing these proposals was published on 1ˢᵗ May, 1962, and distributed widely throughout the country. Members of the public who wished to do so were invited to submit their views, not necessarily restricting themselves to the specific proposals which were outlined in the government paper because members of the public were invited to submit any other views which they considered relevant to the broad issue of the contents of the proposed Republican Constitution. It might be helpful and relevant to mention here that Tanganyika was a multi-party state at that material time. The first phase – if you like – of multi-partysm in independent Tanzania ended in 1965.

When all the views and comments had been collected and analysed, the government published, at the beginning of November of the same year, the resultant bill for submission to Parliament. It was entitled "A Bill for an Act to Declare the Constitution of Tanganyika."

The Bill was subsequently introduced in the House on 23rd September, 1962. In introducing the Bill, the Prime Minister said:

> This Bill, Mr. Speaker, has been prepared in accordance with the proposals contained in government paper No. 1 of 1962.

There is evidence in the Prime Minister's speech to show that some of the earlier government proposals had been modified as a result of comments arising from the public debate. For example, the Prime Minister said:

> Mr. Speaker, the abolition of the power to prorogue the National Assembly is also a departure from the Government paper. We have accepted it after full consideration, in order to emphasise the sovereignty of Parliament.

THE GREEN PAPER OF 1982

In 1981, Chama Cha Mapinduzi (CCM) published a policy document entitled *Mwongozo wa Chama 1981*. There is a section in that document which is devoted to a discussion of desirable changes in the Constitution of the United Republic, starting from page 103 thereof. In order to implement the policy directives which were given in respect of this matter, a "green paper" was issued by the National Executive Committee of CCM setting out proposals for what it considered to be desirable changes in the 1977 Constitution. On that occasion, the initiative was taken by the party (CCM) rather than the government, because of the constitutional arrangements of *party supremacy* which were firmly in place at the material time. Hence it was called a "green paper" rather than a white paper. to differentiate it from government white papers. The party's "Green Paper" set out clearly the proposed changes to the constitution and the reasons thereof. These proposals were again circulated widely throughout the country for general public discussion and comments. The end product was the Fourth Amendment to the Union Constitution Act. 1984. The benefits derived from the public debate were quite noticeable. The original proposals which were circulated by the NEC had not included the very important question of incorporating a Bill of Rights in the Constitution. But as a result of the views expressed by the people, the government of the day readily accepted the proposition that a Bill of Rights should be written into the Constitution. and indeed it was.

These two examples have been cited in order to show that the strategy of a white paper is not at all restrictive, as has been suggested by some observers who have criticised this approach. At least on those two past occasions. there is evidence to show that the public was not prevented from introducing into the discussion other relevant matters which were not included in the original proposals and that some of those new issues were accepted by the government and incorporated in the bills which were submitted to parliament for enactment.

THE PROPOSED GOVERNMENT WHITE PAPER, 1998

When closing the Bunge session on 24th April. 1998 in Dodoma: the Prime Minister announced that the government will issue a white paper at the beginning of June 1998 containing proposals for changes which are to be introduced in the Constitution of the United Republic, in order to take on board the new political situation. the second phase of multi-partyism. which commenced on 1st July. 1992.

A white paper is actually a discussion paper. It is very different, and distinct. from what is known in the British Parliament system as a "Command Paper." A command paper is presented to parliament for information only about the government decisions contained therein. Unlike the white paper. a command paper is not designed for discussion. What the Prime Minister promised in his speech to parliament was a white paper; that is to say, a discussion paper.

I personally believe that the white paper approach is as good a method, as any, for involving the largest number of people in discussing their constitution and what changes should be made to it. When the white paper is published, I strongly suggest that each member of Parliament should actively encourage his constituents to express their views not only on the government proposals, but also on any other relevant issues concerning the constitution, which might have escaped the attention of those who will draft the white paper.

However, a reasonable presumption would be that the government will include in the white paper, all the various issues concerning the constitution which have been raised from time to time by different groups since multi-partysm was restored.

What then should we expect? As we have already seen, the history of constitutional white papers in this country shows that:

a) The government has in every case in the past allowed unrestricted public discussion of its proposals; and

b) The government has also been willing and ready to accept some additional points which were contributed by the public during such debates.

It would appear reasonable therefore to expect that procedurally, these sound precedents will be accepted as binding on the part of the government in its handling of the 1998 constitutional white paper. We should expect further that when the Bill is eventually drafted for presentation to Parliament, it will incorporate the majority views which will have been expressed during the great public debate.

Recommendation for a Discussion Strategy

One viable strategy which I would strongly recommend for ensuring that the public debate of the government proposals is properly organised, is to make arrangements which will ensure that each village assembly, ("mkutano mkuu wa kijiji," which is a local government direct democracy unit) is given an opportunity to discuss the white paper in a formal meeting of that body, where proper minutes will be kept and the decisions of the assembly properly recorded. I believe that this is a very good strategy of involving the people at grass roots level in this important exercise. and I propose to adopt this particular strategy in my own constituency of Ukerewe. I hope other members of Parliament will do likewise in their respective constituencies.

The country has approximately 10.000 village assemblies which are constituted under local government laws. These assemblies are composed of all the adult residents of the village, and they are entitled to meet at least once in every three months. If arrangements can be made so that the white paper becomes the dominant agenda for their very first meetings which will be held after the publication of the forthcoming white paper on constitutional amendments, then some ten thousand village assemblies will have expressed their views in the course of no more than three months. I believe this is a much wider participation and a far more democratic method than calling a single national conference (of a few hundred unelected people) to discuss those important constitutional proposals!

6

MULTI-PARTY DEMOCRACY: THE ONLY POLITICAL MODEL FOR THE NEW MILLENNIUM?

It appears to me that this topic has been deliberately framed in the form of a question, in order that an appropriate answer may be found: but I personally believe that there will be different answers from different people. Some will say "Yes" and some others will say "No"; depending primarily on their personal cultural outlook.

THE CULTURAL ELEMENT IN DEMOCRACY

I am introducing this element of culture at the very beginning of my presentation, because I want to build my main argument around that specific point, starting from the premise that the modern concept of democracy has a distinctive cultural element, which is that modern democracy is in fact a product of Western civilisation. Its roots lie in factors such as their established systems of social pluralism and social justice; their acceptance of the role of civil society; their traditional strong belief in the rule of law; and their long experience in working effectively with elected representative bodies.

HISTORICAL WAVES OF DEMOCRATISATION

An eminent American political scientist has recently identified three historically distinct waves of democratisation, as follows:

> The first long wave of democratisation began in the early 19th century, and led to the triumph of democracy in some 30 countries by 1920. Thereafter, renewed

authoritarianism and the rise of fascism in the 1920s and 1930s reduced the number of democracies in the world to about a dozen by 1942.

The second short wave of democratisation occurred after the 2nd World War, which again increased the number of democracies to somewhat over 30. But this too, was followed by the collapse of democracy in many of those countries.

The third wave of democratisation began in Portugal in the mid 1970s, and has seen democratisation occur much faster and on a scale far surpassing that of the two previous waves. Two decades ago, less than 30 percent of the countries in the world were democratic; now more than 60 per cent have governments produced by some form of open, fair and competitive elections.[1]

The above information is, of course, a helpful survey of the past. But the topic which is before us now calls for a discussion of the future of democracy. We are asked to look into the next millennium and make a reasonable forecast as to whether multi-party democracy will be the only political model for that millennium.

The great achievement of the third wave of democratisation appears to be the general acceptance of the universality of democracy in the Western countries; as well as the promotion of its manifestations in non-western societies. In recent years, for example, many Africa countries, have made successful transitions from single party systems to multi-partysm. Thus, if I may return briefly to the cultural element in democracy, the following question becomes immediately relevant. To what extent will this kind of democracy, being essentially a product of the West, remain sustainable in non-Western societies in the new millennium?

This question inevitably raises the issue of the *meaning* of democracy to people of different cultures.

IDENTIFICATION OF DEMOCRACY WITH ELECTIONS

There is strong practical evidence that currently, the dominant trend is to define democracy almost entirely in terms of elections; whereby democracy is viewed as a means of constituting governmental authority and making that authority accountable to the citizens. This is achieved by ensuring that the "rulers" are selected periodically by the votes of the "ruled" through free and fair elections, in which virtually the entire adult population is eligible to vote.

Hence, a modern nation-state is deemed to have a democratic political system only if its government is selected through fair, honest and periodic elections in which candidates freely compete for votes. According to this definition, elections are the *essence* of democracy. From this follow other implied characterics of the democratic system, principally that free, fair and competitive elections are only possible where there is freedom of assembly and speech. More importantly, its is presumed that these characteristics can only be guaranteed by a multi-party system, where people can choose betwen competing political parties representing different shades of opinion.

However, evidence is available to show that whereas in Western political culture, it is recognised and accepted that the fundamental features of a political party are organisation and discipline; i.e. organisation of support in the country generally, and discipline of its members in parliament: this is not always the case in other non-Western cultures, as for instance in Haiti, where it has been reported that "party politics and party discipline are practically unknown in Haiti." Parties in that country "are often small bands, led by egomaniacs and held together by patronage." Inside Parliament, "party affiliation does not always guarantee agreement. The government of President Rene Preval, in office since February 1966, cannot get its programmes through Parliament, because that body often fails to reach a quorum, and acts capriciously when it does, even though most of its seats are held by members of the president's Lavalas movement"2

SHORTCOMINGS OF ELECTORAL DEMOCRACY
Taking elections and its associated characteristics as the essence of democracy actually does not give us the perfect model we are looking for. There are two reasons for this. The first is that although electoral democracies will indeed produce elected governments, but it is still possible in some cases for such elected governments to be seriously lacking in the other essential safeguards for individual rights and liberties. These safeguards include rules which restrict the powers of the executive: the presence of independent judiciaries to uphold the rule of law: and rules for the protection of individual rights of expression, association, religious belief, and political participation: the existence of mechanisms for the protection of the rights of minorities: and the presence of effective

controls to prevent the people who are in power from manipulating the electoral process in their own favour; and provisions for minimum government control of the media.

The second reason is that there have indeed been situations whereby free elections have led to the victory of political leaders or groups that subsequently threaten the maintenance of democracy itself. There are numerous examples of elected governments which have often acted in arbitrary and undemocratic ways: suppressing their opponents, paying little attention to individual rights, and curtailing the freedom of the press.

In some particular cases, especially in non-western multi-party electoral cultures, this has often been a direct reaction of the party in power to an absurd situation created by the so-called "Savimbi theory of elections." This theory, which is associated with Mr Savimbi of Angola, states that "if you go into an election, you must win. If you don't win you have been cheated." So you must refuse to recognise the results of that election, and immediately start fighting against the winning party, through a variety of acts of commission or omission; which in turn forces the ruling party to respond by using state power to fight back.

As a result of this, some people have begun to question this blanket identification of democracy with multi-party elections. At a Global Coalition for Africa Conference held in Nov. 1995 on the theme of "Africa's Future and the World," many of the participants underscored the importance of going beyond the political parties by involving the larger society in the democratisation process. While recognising the importance of multi-partysm to promote political competition and facilitate representation, that conference also emphasised the need for a strong civil society in building and sustaining democracy, as well as in acting as a check on government. The conference cautioned that multi-partysm does not automatically lead to democracy.

THE DANGERS OF ETHNICITY AND RELIGION

In a number of countries, election campaigns have tended to provide politicians with the incentive to make appeals of an ethnic or religious nature in order to obtain the most votes. Such appeals inevitably exacerbate tribal or religious divisions within the country, and most often result in civil strife.

President Mkapa of the United Republic of Tanzania recently highlighted this particular problem in the following terms:

> In making the transition to multi-party politics, we always had the apprehension that it could lead to a resurgence of tribal and religious sentiments and differences among our people, thereby undermining the national identify and cohesion we have worked so hard to develop and nurture. But thanks to the political maturity of most of our people, these fears never materialised. Despite the verbal and written diatribes, amplified too often by a too free press, there has never really been a serious threat to the political unity and cohesion of our country, as well as the peace and concord which our people have now become used to.[3]

In neighbouring Kenya, a keen observer of the political situation there has commented that:

> there is evidence that the present opposition in Kenya suffers from acute ethnic inclination, as they are carefully moulded to divide the country along ethnic lines; and as such cannot be relied upon as proper vehicles of popular, participatory democracy for social change.[4]

NATIONAL UNITY AND ELECTORAL DEMOCRACY

The overriding importance of national unity in many of the developing countries may make multi-party electoral democracy unworkable. It is the need for national unity which led most of the newly independent countries of Africa to adopt the single-party political system during the 1960s.

And this is by no means surprising, because another look at history shows that historically, democratic pluralism came into being with the gradual acceptance of toleration in the aftermath of the religious wars which ravaged Europe during the sixteenth and seventeenth centuries. By and large, until the seventeenth century, diversity was considered a source of discord and disorder, which often led to the downfall of nation-states; while unanimity was regarded as the necessary foundation of any polity. But from then on, the opposite attitude gradually took hold, whereby unanimity came to be viewed with suspicion. This radical change of perspective is said to have provided the route through which present day electoral democracy was brought about, based as it is, on tolerance of dissent and diversity. These two are regarded as the central values that enrich individuals as well as their polities, which are achievable through tolerance, bargaining and compromise among rival political groups.

The countries of Africa and elsewhere, which placed great emphasis on national unity at independence in the 1960s and actually continue to do so to the present day, may be considered to be at the same stage as that which existed in Europe prior to the seventeenth century: when diversity was considered to be a source of discord and disorder, and unity was regarded to be the necessary foundation of any polity. And, who knows, the new millennium may well see a resurgence of these attitudes in the relevant countries: with consequent influences on their choice of an appropriate political system, which could possibly be other than multi-partysm.

MULTI-PARTY DEMOCRACY: THE ONLY MODEL FOR THE NEW MILLENNIUM?

In the light of the foregoing observations, we may now attempt a possible answer to the question whether multi-partysm is the only political model for the new millennium. Let us first consider the options which are available. The Constitution of the Republic of Uganda is hugely helpful in this particular regard. Section 69 of that Constitution provides that:

69 (1) The people of Uganda shall have the right to choose and adopt a political system of their choice through free and fair elections, or referanda.

(2) The political system referred to in clause (1) shall include:
  a) The movement political system (which is broad based, inclusive and non-partisan).
  b) The multi-party political system.
  c) Any other democratic and representative system.

As can be seen, the Uganda Constitution fully recognises that apart from the multi-party system, there are other viable political systems which are available; and currently that country has chosen the "movement political system," which presumably will take them into the next millennium. In one way therefore, the Uganda Constitution has provided one answer to our question whether multi-partysm is the only political model for the new millennium, by asserting clearly that there are other viable models.

Multi-partysm is currently the most fashionable model of democracy, because it is part of the historical third wave of democratisation. It is obviously not possible to predict whether or not there will be other waves in the new millennium, which might either produce new and different models of democracy; or create increased acceptability of some of the current options, such as the Ugandan movement political system; which can safely be regarded as a no-party system.

CONCLUSION

As has already been stated, the main achievement of the third wave of democratisation has been to ensure the universality of democracy in Western countries, and to promote its manifestations in other non-Western countries. Therefore one possible answer to our question is that this third wave will indeed be sustained in the new millennium, as the only universal political model.

But multi-partysm is based on the principle that a political party is a grouping together of like-minded individuals who broadly share the same vision or ideology; and the same approach with regard to the management of the nation's social and economic development. Various such groups then compete periodically in free elections in order to be given a chance by the electorate to form the government.

There are two points which are worth making here. First, as we have pointed out in discussing the dangers of ethnicity and religion in politics, where political parties consist of like-minded persons only in the sense that they belong to the same tribe or religion, this not only radically changes the whole character as well as the fundamental objectives of multi-partysm as a political model; but, even worse, threatens the unity and solidarity of the nation.

Secondly, it has now been established that in certain political jurisdictions, people seek to join a particular political party not because they like its ideology, or vision, or its development strategies, but they do so for entirely selfish motives. Their basic ambition is to get elected to parliament or to a local government authority; so they join a political party which they will use as a vehicle which will enable them to enter

Parliament or become members of a local representative body, and for no any other reason. In both these situations, it may be difficult for electoral democracy, which is based on multi-partysm to continue to flourish in those countries whose cultural environment renders them vulnerable to these deficiencies.

Lastly, if it can be shown that in the absence of competing ideologies or sharply conflicting opinions among the population, free and fair elections can still be held successfully where competition is between individuals rather than political parties; and governments of national unity can be successfully formed as a result of such elections, (as happened in Uganda); then multi-partysm will loose its monopoly as the only political model in the new millennium. My own prediction is that multi-partysm will most probably remain the only universally *fashionable* political model: but will not be the only *functional* model.

Endnotes

1. Samuel P. Huntington: "After Twenty Years: The Future of the Third Wave" *Journal for Democracy*. October 1997 p.4.
2. Jean Germain Gros: "Haiti's Flagging Transition," *The Journal of Democracy*, October 1997. p.100.
3. President Benjamin Mkapa's Speech at a New Year Sherry Party for Heads of Diplomatic Missions in Dar es Salaam, Jan. 1996.
4. Ocholla: "Forces that Militate Against Opposition" in *The People*, November 1996.

7

THE TANGANYIKA (CONSTITUTION) ORDER IN COUNCIL, 1961

COULD NO MINISTRY BE CREATED WITHOUT THE CONSENT OF THE NATIONAL ASSEMBLY?

I wish to return to the constitutional debate which was initiated by M. Masatu & M. Mkucha in the *Sunday Observer* of October 19th, 1997 about the contents of the Independence Constitution of Tanganyika, 1961. The said authors had claimed in their article that "in the Independence Constitution, the President could not create ministries without the consent of the National Assembly."

I challenged that statement by saying that "there was no such provision in the Independence Constitution." I based my statement on the fact that I was the Clerk of the National Assembly at the material time. Because in that capacity, I would certainly have been the first person to know whenever the consent of the National Assembly was being sought for the creation of any ministry. But in fact no such request for parliament's consent was ever submitted to the National Assembly during the whole of the period when that Constitution was in force, namely from 9th December 1961 to 9th December, 1962.

My statement was in turn challenged by Masatu & Mkucha, who quoted the relevant provision of the Tanganyika (Constitution) Order in Council, 1961, to prove their point that ministries could not be created under that Constitution without the consent of Parliament. The debate was suspended at that stage because I got completely caught up in

Dodoma, first with the Bunge end-of-the year session; which was followed immediately by the CCM congress. I am now back in circulation and would like to complete my side of the story.

There is no dispute regarding the wording of section 42(2) of the second scheduled to the Tanganyika. (Constitution) Order in Council, 1961. G.N. 415 published on 1/12/1961) reads as follows:

> There shall be, in addition to the Office of Prime Minister, such other offices of Minister as may be established by Parliament, or subject to the provisions of any Act of Parliament, by the Governor-General acting in accordance with the advice of the Prime Minister.

A correct reading of that section suggests that it makes provision for two distinct options, either:

a) Ministries may be established by resolution of Parliament; or
b) They may be established by the Governor-General acting in accordance with the advice of the Prime Minister.

The wording of this section actually confirms my earlier challenge to Masatu & Mkucha, who had claimed that "in the Independence Constitution of Tanganyika, the President could not create Ministries without the consent of the National Assembly." That paraphrasing by Masatu & Mkucha of the relevant section of the said constitution makes it appear to be a mandatory provision: when in fact it was not. The relevant section 42(2), as already quoted above, uses the word "may" and not "shall." It reads thus "... as may be established by Parliament, or ...." As can be seen, the wording is only enabling, not mandatory. That was precisely my reason for saying that "there was no such mandatory provision in the Independence Constitution."

I may perhaps add here that the reference by Massatu & Mkucha to the "President" in this context was also misplaced, for there was no office of the President under the Independence Constitution. The highest constitutional authority was the Governor-General, who represented Her Majesty the Queen of Great Britain and Northern Ireland, and Head of State of Tanganyika.

For the avoidance of doubt, it should be noted that it was the latter option alone, (i.e. creation of ministries by the Governor-General) which was adopted for use throughout the period when the Tanganyika Independence Constitution was in force. Ministries were on all occasions during that period, created by the Governor-General by notices in the official gazette. The National Assembly was never, at any time, asked to establish ministries.

The first creation of ministries under the Independence Constitution was done by the Governor-General through Government Notice No. 447 published on 15/12/1961. The said notice established the very first set of ministries with effect from the ninth day of December 1961 (independence day) as follows:

Minister for Finance;
Minister for Legal Affairs;
Minister for Health & Labour;
Minister for Home Affairs;
Minister for Communications, Power and Works;
Minister for Agriculture;
Minister for Commerce and Industry;
Minister for Commerce and Industry;
Minister for Education;
Minister without Portfolio;
Minister for Lands, Forests & Wildlife;
Minister for Local Government.

Indeed, this procedure of creating ministries by direction of the head of state was common practice in other countries' constitutions as well. For example:

II (1) There shall be a Council of ministries in and for Kenya, which, subject to
sect. 16 of this order shall consist of such number of ministries as may
be prescribed by her Majesty, by instructions to the Governor through a
Secretary of State.

In Tanganyika, this continued to be the practice until the said Order in Council was replaced by the Republican Constitution of Tanganyika which came into force on 9th December, 1962, and made the following unambiguous provision [section 11(2) thereof]:

There shall be such other offices of Minister as the President may, from time to time by instrument under the public seal, establish.

In conclusion, I would like to underscore the point that there was no mandatory requirement under the Tanganyika Independence Constitution of 1961, for the head of state to obtain parliamentary approval for the creation of any ministry. Such establishment of ministries by resolution of parliament was provided in that constitution only as an option. But that option was never used. And it was probably never intended to be used! Considering the fact that the said constitution was made in London by Her Majesty's Government, for implementation in Tanganyika by Her Majesty's own representative, the Governor-General, it must have been the firm wish of the framers of that constitution that, despite the provision of another option, ministries should in fact be established only by Order of the Governor-General. And so it came to pass.

8

THE NEED FOR THE GENERAL PUBLIC TO BE
EDUCATED ABOUT THE CONSTITUTION

Dear Mr. Editor,

The people who commented on my innocent remarks concerning the need for raising public awareness regarding the provisions of our country's constitution (*The Guardian*, Thursday, March 27th 1997) have sadly missed the point.

All of them seem to direct their energies to challenging a point which I did not make at all. Their assertion is that "the current Constitution is unfair because it is biased in favor of the ruling party, CCM. Therefore it needs overhauling.' But that was certainly not the point of my lecture at Kagunguli Secondary School. The purpose of my lecture was to explain how parliament works, a topic which is an important part of the civics syllabus for secondary schools in Tanzania. Nevertheless, my response to their challenge is as follows:

a) If it is indeed that the Constitution is unfair, then that only helps to strengthen my basic argument, which is that the general public should be made aware of the so-called bad provisions of the constitution, so that they may effectively join the campaign for the removal of any such bad provisions from our constitution.

b) Whether or not the current Constitution contains some unfair provisions, it still remains the country's Constitution, until it is changed through the normal parliamentary processes. The relevant legal books of authority say that 'ignorance of the law is no defense.' Therefore any positive initiative which is aimed at reducing the peoples' ignorance of the law' through a program of public legal education is definitely commendable. That such knowledge is presently lacking was easily demonstrated by some of my critics, who challenged what they imagined was a constitutional provision, which empowers the President to detain a person without a court trial.

In fact, there is no such provision in our Constitution. The President's powers of detention are enshrined in a different law, namely the Preventive Detention Act. Public education about the contents of our Constitution will definitely help to eradicate such unnecessary ignorance. Finally, and for avoidance of any further confusion, I would like to restate my position as follows:

What I actually said in my Kagunguli Secondary School lecture was that the general public should be enlightened about the provisions of the constitution of our country. For it is the awareness so created which will enable the people to make informed decision about the fairness or otherwise of our constitution.

However, for those who feel that there are certain provisions of the constitution which are unfair or biased in favor of the ruling party, CCM, my own challenge to them is that they should ask their party's members of parliament to table the necessary amendment bill for discussion in parliament, for parliament is the sole authority for amending or changing the country's constitution. If such an amendment bill is presented to parliament, it will at first enable the public at large to identify the so-called bad provisions of the Constitution, and presumably enable them to join the campaign for their removal. In my opinion, that will be a much more productive exercise than merely complaining in general terms about the Constitution being unfair.

9

SIMPLE MINDS DISCUSS PEOPLE

Dear Mr Editor,

I was greatly disappointed by your editorial of May 1-7, 1997, primarily because you too have succumbed to the evil habit of discussing the *person* who proposes an idea, instead of discussing the *idea* which he proposes. Please remember:

> Simple minds discuss *people*.
> Ordinary minds discuss *events*.
> Great minds discuss *ideas*.

What I did was to propose an idea, namely that of proportional representation. But instead of discussing the pros and cons of that *idea*, you simply jumped to the conclusion, which you summarised in your heading: "Msekwa, you are wrong." This is disappointing!! Furthermore, you have completely misunderstood the reason for my suggesting proportional representation. It is certainly not for the purpose of finding a solution to the problem of absenteeism in parliament.

Such absenteeism does not depend at all on the electoral system which is in use. It depends on a variety of other factors, including attendance at parliamentary committee meetings; consultations with people from their constituencies visiting their MPs in Dodoma; or with government ministers trying to find solutions to the problems of their constituencies;

etc. This is in fact the position in many other parliaments all over the world. The logic of it is that members of parliament should not be equated to students sitting in a class room, who must be there all the time to listen to their teacher. There is no such teacher in parliament who must be listened to. On the other hand, provided they are within the precincts of the parliamentary buildings, members of parliament can follow debates which are taking place in the House, through a specially designed sound transmission equipment. Hence their absence from the chamber itself is of minor importance, so long as they are carrying out their other parliamentary duties and responsibilities elsewhere in the complex of parliament buildings.

Finally, I wish to repeat my plea, that people should discuss the *idea* which has been proposed: and refrain from discussing the person who proposed that idea. Let me also restate my proposal, which is that the proportional representation electoral system is better suited to the needs of Tanzania than the "First-past-the post system." I am not saying that the proportional representation system has no problems of its own. Naturally, no system can be perfect. I should perhaps make it clear that what I am advocating is a mixture of the two systems, as they have it in Germany. I have also in mind the electoral systems of New Zealand, which is called the *mixed member proportional representation system*, which is also a combination of 'first-past-the post' and proportional representation systems.

I will be grateful if you will publish my clarification of this matter, as it will help to focus the debate on this crucial issue in the right direction, i.e. the debate should focus on the proposal itself, and never on the person who makes that proposal.

This is a very important principle, because otherwise there will be no democracy in parliament, if the proposals which are submitted by the opposition MPs were to be rejected by the ruling party MPs merely because the said proposals came from the opposition! We should all fight against that undemocratic culture of "simple minds" which discuss people, and work diligently for the development of the culture of "great minds," which discuss idea.

10

PARLIAMENTARY DEMOCRACY IN TANZANIA: PRESENT SITUATION AND FUTURE REFORMS*1

We have now gone through one and a half years since the first multi-party elections of 1995. At the end of the first 100 days I made an assessment of how we had faired so far. It was noted that the following progress had been achieved:

1) A new Bunge building had been acquired in Dodoma and suitably equipped for the parliamentary plenary sessions. Reasons for acquiring a new building are:
   a) To accommodate the increased number of MPs,
   b) To house the parliament in a building which did not belong to any of the political parties,
   c) To implement the national decision of making Dodoma the new capital: by initially making Dodoma the Legislative Capital, similar to Cape Town in South Africa.

2) All the parliamentary committees had been appointed and given a truly multi-party appearance, by ensuring that a reasonable number of opposition m embers were placed on each committee, including the sensitive Defence and Security Committee. But at that time,

---

*1 Presentation made to the donor Community – 5th June, 1997

after only 100 days. Parliament had had only one business session, in January/February 1996. Since then, we have had five more sessions. One of which was the Budget session of 1996/97. The other four were almost entirely devoted to passing legislation.

In the light of the experience gained during that period, it is now possible for me to make another assessment, of the progress we are steadily making in operating a multi-party parliament, and to highlight what I consider to be some of the problems which need to be addressed, both in the short term and long term. For the purpose of today's discussion, I have identified the following two specific procedural weaknesses which I observed during this period, which I have already taken the necessary remedial action. These are:

a) That the parliamentary committees were being rendered inefective by requiring them to meet simultaneously with the plenary sessions of Bunge. This was previously dictated by budgetary considerations, whereby it was considered that it would effect considerable expenditure savings. But it has now been agreed by the Government to fund the committees separately. We have accordingly now established a new practice, through a Speaker's ruling, that the committees will normally be programmed to meet the week before the ensuing plenary session of Bunge, instead of during the Bunge session itself.

b) That the "Shadow Cabinet" members were manifestly disadvantaged during the last budget session, in the sense that they were being asked to present the position of the opposition on the budget proposals, when in fact they had not been given sufficient opportunity to study the budget proposals before hand. I have now rectified that by issuing another Speaker's ruling, which enables all the shadow ministers to attend all the pre-budget meetings of the Finance and Economic Committee of Parliament, which are routinely held for the purpose of scrutinising closely the budget proposals, before they are presented to Parliament. This ruling is already effective, and the shadow ministers are in fact currently sitting in the on-going two-week meeting of the Finance and Economic Committee precisely for that purpose.

This is part of a determined effort on my part, to remove any impediments to the effective participation by the opposition in the work of our new multi-party parliament. These rulings will subsequently be incorporated in the Standing Orders of the House.

With regard to the institutional problems, I wish to mention the following:

a) The inadequacy of the physical facilities;
b) Insufficiency of the normal standard working tools;
c) Limited parliamentary experience for the majority of MPs as well as the staff of the Speaker's office.

With regard to physical facilities, fortunately I am today in a position to say that the partitioning of the office block of the Bunge House has finally been given the go-ahead, in an official letter from the Principal Secretary PMO, to the Secretary of the LAPF Governing Council, dated 10th April, 1997. That letter clarifies a point which had hitherto been unclear, namely whether the government's intention was to purchase the building as it is, i.e. without office partitioning, and do the partitioning itself; or whether they wanted LAPF to do the partitioning and sell it to the government in its completed form. That letter has confirmed the latter option as being the government's intention.

That clarification has now enabled LAPF to go ahead with the job. This in turn will enable the donors to undertake the provisions of furniture and equipment for the offices as previously agreed.

But while I am still on this question of the Bunge building, I would also like to mention another thing, which is the need for improving our cafeteria services. The Bunge kitchen is ill-equipped, and is actually still located in the old building, which is rented: and worse still, it uses charcoal or fuel! There is a great need for appropriate new kitchen equipment to be procured and installed in the new Bunge house.

Insufficiency of the normal standard working tools refers to equipment such as computers and photo-copying machines, for the rapid production of documents, particularly for the *Hansard* Department, and the Bunge Library. The computers currently being used by the Hansard Department are already dilapidated and obsolete. They are IBM models which are not expandable. They do not suffice the needs; hence, they need to be replaced urgently. Furthermore, both the Hansard Department and the Library, need to be provided with heavy-duty photo-copiers. As you will have seen already, most of the legislation which is brought to Parliament is *amending* legislation for the purpose of amending numerous old laws. It is of course essential for MPs to have copies of the old law which is amended, so that they can see the effect of the proposed amendments. But the facilities for reproducing these old laws is sadly lacking.

On the other hand the Hansard department is responsible for reproducing those documents which are laid on the table of the House, but are sometimes not delivered to the Clerks' Office in sufficient number for distribution to all MPs. They need to be reproduced.

Hence, both the Hansard and Library Departments need heavy duty photo-copying machines, to improve the services which they are required to deliver. Actually, in the long run, the Hansard Department needs a printer, which will enable it to be independent of the Government Press.

By way of illustration of the gravity of this problem, I may mention that no Hansard has been printed since April 1996, which means that the official records of a whole year's work are not yet available to MPs and the public libraries, and all the other recepients of that important document.

This is obviously a great obstacle because, for example, the House is soon entering its 1997/98 budget session, when they have no record of what transpired in the 1996/97 budget. The MPs will therefore be unable to make references to ministerial promises made during the last budget. That clearly reduces the effectiveness of Parliament, and ought to be remedied. I am grateful that UNDP has agreed to provide the remedy.

Both the Library and the Hansard Department need to be properly equipped for the speedy processing of parliamentary proceedings. Parliament's printing needs, however, go far beyond the production of Hansard. As we continue to consolidate and strengthen our services, there will be increased demand for printing of parliamentary documents like sessional papers, reports of parliamentary committees both standing and select committees, private members' bills and motions; and a host of other documentation. This is is what justifies my earlier reference to the need for a complete printing unit for the Hansard Department.

The issue of limited experience of parliamentary practices and procedures disadvantages both the MPs themselves, and the staff of the Speaker's office. The solution to this problem lies in the provision of training opportunities for both categories; including training workshops and seminars; and the chance of exposure study to other parliaments.

Mr Chairman, As I said in my interview with the *Business Times Newspaper* which was published last Friday, I firmly believe that multi-partyism is here to stay; and parliament is the one basic institution which gives credence to the successful functioning of this system.

Therefore as Speaker of the House during this historic initial period of the transition, I feel I have a moral duty to lay the necessary firm foundation, upon which a properly functioning and effective multi-party parliament will be built.

Your Excellencies, I thank you very much for you kind attention.

11

PARLIAMENTARY DEBATES ARE NOT FOR ENTERTAINMENT

I read with considerable interest. Wilson Bukholi's article which was published in the *Sunday Observer* of October 12, 1997, entitled "Is our Parliament losing its esteemed prestige and dignity?"

In that article. Bukholi argues in favour of a "Yes" answer. And he is basically right, because the whole question of general public discontent with the performance of their MPs is a matter which often comes up for discussion in many meetings of Commonwealth parliamentarians in different parts of the Commonwealth. Hence this is a general problem affecting nearly all parliaments. It certainly is not confined to Tanzania alone. The essence of the problem lies in the following basic question: "What exactly does the Tanzanian public expect from their parliamentarians?"

Bukholi quotes a statement made by a senior journalist to the effect that "very little of public interest comes out of Parliament these days;" while another journalist is reported to have said that "discussions in parliament have become dull." In my view, these comments seem to point to a desire for entertainment. So the vital questions are: Does the Tanzanian public really expect to be entertained by parliamentary debates? What in fact is the perceived role of MPs? Do they perform that role satisfactorily?

Members of the public may indeed be entitled to some entertainment from the debates of their representatives in parliament; but it must be emphasised that unlike public rallies. the primary function of Parliament is to give serious consideration to a variety of proposals which are regularly submitted by the government of the day for parliament's approval. The bulk of these proposals relate to legislation, or the making of laws for our country; while budget proposals constitute the other major category of government proposals which require parliamentary debate and approval.

THERE IS NO ROOM FOR ENTERTAINMENT IN SERIOUS BUSINESS

Legislative proposals are mostly technical in nature, and hence they do not lend themselves easily to entertaining discussion or debate on the floor of that august House. Similarly, government budgetary proposals are very serious matters of utmost importance for the good governance and well-being of our nation. The famous slogan of "no taxation without representation" reminds us of the urgent need for our parliamentarians to undertake the task of discussing government taxation proposals with all the seriousness it deserves. It is therefore unfair for anyone to expect MPs to be making entertaining speeches when they are discussing such important and serious business as making the laws of our country; or approving taxation and expenditure proposals submitted to them by the government.

It is a truism that any serious discussion is necessarily dull. It may well be very lively as far as the participants themselves are concerned; but it will be made of rather hard stuff which will generally appear to be dull and uninteresting to an external observer. Take, for example some serious discussion which takes place in a University tutorial class. It may be lively and intellectually rewarding to the participating academicians; but outside observers, including journalist who are not specialist in that particular field, will easily find it dull and uninteresting.

This is what usually happens when parliamentarians get down to the business of discussing government legislative proposals, otherwise known as government Bills. Outside people listening to the relevant debate will most likely regard it as dull and uninteresting. This is because many people usually enjoy the performance of politicians at public rallies. And, because their MPs are basically politicians, members of the public tend to expect the same performance from them when they are debating issues in Parliament. But it should be noted that there is a world of difference between these two forums. Whereas public rallies have no rules of procedure to be followed, parliamentary debates are strictly regulated by established rules of procedure known as Standing Orders. For example, whereas at a public rally. a politician may talk for as long as he likes about virtually anything under the sun, and may even make remarks whose authenticity is highly doubtful: the parliamentary rules are prohibitive of any such conduct. A member of parliament is allowed to speak only on the particular topic which is under discussion at the material time; and he or she must never introduce any fraudulent material by making statements which are false or untrue. For this reason alone, the entertaining which is normally generated at public rallies has no place whatsoever in parliamentary proceedings.

THE PUBLIC RIGHTLY EXPECTS VIGOROUS CHALLENGES TO THE GOVERNMENT

I am of course aware that what many interested Tanzanians would like to hear from the floor of parliament is a vigorous challenge to the proposals which are submitted by the government; a challenge which preferably should be spiced by an occasional rejection of some of these proposals. So they get thoroughly disappointed when this does not happen. Hence, as far as they are concerned, the debates become dull and uninteresting.

But there is a very valid explanation for this state of affairs, which is as follows: There are two fundamental principles which are the foundation of the parliamentary system of government which is distinctly different from, and should not be confused with, the presidential system. The first of these two principles is that in the parliamentary system of government, government ministers must be appointed only from among the members of parliament. This means that the ministers are at the same time members of parliament, elected in the same manner as all the other MPs, and being answerable in similar manner as all the other MPs, and being answerable in similar manner to the people of Tanzania. This is because they too, like the other MPs, have to constantly think of the need to fight and win the next election. This naturally restrains them from making any ghastly or "anti-people" proposals and submitting them to parliament for approval! Because of that, government proposals are of necessity prepared very carefully, thereby leaving no opportunity for a "vigorous" challenge from the other parliamentarians, including those of the opposition camp. This is how the government ensures its survival in office; i.e. by submitting to parliament only those proposals which appear to have a reasonable chance of being accepted there. Because under multi-partysm, a serious defeat in parliament may cause the removal of the government from office.

The second principle is that a parliamentary system of government is essentially "government by the majority political party." This means that whereas all the qualifying political parties are given the opportunity to compete for people's votes during a general election, it is the winning party alone which takes the entire prize of that competition, namely, the right to form the government. In other words, it is a "winner-take-all" situation. Naturally, the winning party wants to retain its prize for the whole five-year life of parliament. For that reason, they will strive to avoid doing anything which might bring about the loss of that precious prize before the end of their term.

MULTI-PARTYISM PUTS GREAT EMPHASIS ON PARTY DISCIPLINE

It is therefore absolutely native for anyone to expect that the majority ruling party members of parliament will do anything which might result in their government's proposals being defeated. It is a moral obligation for them to support the government of their party on the floor of the House. Hence the reason for the concept of party discipline and its application in all multi-party parliaments.

These are some of the rules of multi-party political competition which we must now learn to accept, because that is the *modus operandi* of any multi-party parliament. Such rules were of course non-existent during the long period of the one party system of government. Therefore they are new to most Tanzanians, and this may be one of the factors contributing to the general public's cynical view that "nothing interesting comes out of parliament these days."

THE ROLE OF THE MEDIA IN MAKING PARLIAMENT LOSE ITS DIGNITY

As in so many other things where the power of the mass media can make itself felt, the same media can also shape the public image of parliament, either positively or negatively, depending on how parliamentary proceedings are reported therein.

In the course of any one parliamentary sitting day many words are spoken, and numerous comments are made by individual members of parliament. The majority of them will have made quite serious contributions to the on-going debate. But perhaps in conformity with the proverbial "one rotten fish spoils the whole basket," one or two publicity-seeking MPs may deliberately choose to make some absurd remarks, which are entirely unrepresentative of the general mood of the House as a whole. And yet, for some obscure reason, the press will pick up these individual remarks and sell them to the public as if they were the consensus opinion of the whole Parliament! Naturally, because of the absurdity of those remarks, the dignity of Parliament will have been dented.

We have already seen a few examples of this in the last two years since the present multi-party parliament was elected in October 1995. For example, there was the case of one MP who in one parliamentary debate, advanced a purely personal opinion that all the MPs should upon being elected, be paid an allowance of one million shillings each, to enable them to buy appropriate clothing which is commensurate with their newly acquired high status. Surprisingly, this was quoted widely and repeatedly in the press, being fraudulently misrepresented as if it was a decision of the whole parliament; thereby creating a very negative public impression of parliament itself as an institution; as well as painting a similarly negative picture of MPs as persons who spend their time in parliament discussing their own personal needs, instead of addressing the general problems of the whole community.

The other example is the recent event of one MP marrying a school girl in Dodoma, which was given such extraordinary publicity that it almost created the impression that all MPs were now concentrating on marrying school girls, thereby causing some painful embarrassment to the innocent majority of MPs, and considerably damaging their reputation. It is this kind of mis-information which will almost certainly lower the esteem and dignity of Parliament in the eyes of the public. Bukholi's article, presumably unwittingly, makes the same unfortunate mis-representation.

In this article, Bukholi picks out an isolated remark which he claims was made by a member of parliament, that "Tanzanian male parliamentarians cannot have their beer or drink it without the company of their female colleagues." I have personally searched through, but have not been able to find it anywhere in the Hansard, which is the verbatim report of all parliamentary proceedings. Therefore if such a remark was made at all, then it must have been made jokingly in one of the weekly Saturday seminars for members of parliament, and not in Parliament itself.

But even if it had been made on the floor of Parliament itself, it would surely be unreasonable to claim that one funny joke like that can make the whole institution of parliament lose its dignity! Indeed, as the proverb says, "beauty is in the eye of the beholder." The claim that our Parliament is losing its dignity just because of such isolated light-hearted jokes, seems to be based entirely on purely subjective individual considerations.

CONCLUSION

It is therefore hereby submitted, in conclusion, that if it is indeed the general view that "parliament is losing its esteem, prestige and dignity," then this view is probably based on a misunderstanding of the functioning of the parliamentary system under multi-partysm. The public is advised that multi-partysm is a competitive system, with fixed but transparent rules of the game. According to these rules, the members of each party which is represented in Parliament must always act together as one team. The ruling party MPs in particular, must act together in support of all the proposals which are submitted to parliament by the government of their own party; in order to avoid the possibility of those measures being defeated on the floor of the House.

If this is what, in the eyes of the public, makes our parliamentary debates "dull and uninteresting" as has been suggested in Bukholi's article, then we now know the true reason for the existence of such state of affairs. In whatever country, where the electorate has given one political party an overwhelming majority in parliament, as happened in Tanzania in October 1995 and in Britain in May 1997 (to name only two countries out of many), expectations of parliamentary "vigorous challenges" to government proposals are largely misplaced. Our on-going parliamentary civic education which was recently initiated by the Speaker's Office, is intended to help create a better understanding of these issues. It should perhaps be mentioned, as a point of further clarification, that the ruling party MPs (in all multi-party parliaments) have their own internal caucuses, whose rules permit them to hotly criticise their government in the meetings of their caucuses, and even force it to withdraw an unpopular proposal. But that particular aspects of the conduct of business in multi-party parliaments cannot be adequately discussed within the ambit of this article, for it is broad enough to require separate treatment. It will, however, be well covered in our parliament civic education programme, which is already being implemented.

12

THE DOCTRINE OF CONTEMPT OF PARLIAMENT
AND ITS APPLICATION IN TANZANIA

INTRODUCTION

The doctrine of contempt of parliament remains largely unknown here in Tanzania; whereas, on the other hand, the identical doctrine of contempt of court is much better known to the general public. This is mainly because of the extensive network of the courts which covers practically all parts of the country, thus enabling many more people to get reasonable exposure to the court system and its proceedings, either directly as litigants or witnesses, or indirectly as interested observers of court proceedings in their respective areas of domicile.

In contrast, it is a very tiny fraction of the population which has ever been exposed to parliamentary proceedings because these have always taken place in one fixed location, previously at the Karimjee Hall in Dar es Salaam, and presently at Bunge House, Dodoma. Furthermore, during the 30 years of the one party political system, parliament was effectively side-lined by the party to the extent that not many people paid any attention to its proceedings. Now however, with the adoption of the multi-party political system, parliament has rightfully regained its centre-piece position as the true representative of the sovereignty of the people. Consequently, its proceedings have become the focus of public attention.

This chapter is intended to enlighten the public regarding the existence of the offence which is known as contempt of parliament, and its consequences on any person who might be convicted of the commission of that offence. This is important because any member of the public who, for one reason or another, might be involved in the business of parliament, may find himself charged with the commission of such an offence. Hence, it is important for members of the public to be informed about what exactly constitutes the offence of contempt of parliament, for their own protection. But before we embark on a detailed discussion of the doctrine of contempt of parliament, it will be helpful, for purposes of comparison, to revisit its more familiar counterpart doctrine of contempt of court.

CONTEMPT OF COURT

Every person who is familiar with the Court system is aware of the offence known as contempt of court. Mr Justice B.D. Chipeta, in his book titled *"A Magistrate's Manual,"* at p.219, describes that offence in the following terms:

> Nothing should be done or omitted to be done in the Court or out of Court, which shows disrespect to, or with references to, the presiding judge or magistrate, or which obstructs or interferes or in any way hinders the due course of justice.

Judge Chipeta explains further that in order to ensure that judicial proceedings are conducted in an atmosphere of seriousness, serenity and dignity, "judges and magistrates are clothed with the very important power of punishing such transgressors summarily for contempt of court."

With regard to the procedure for punishing that kind of offence, Judge Chipeta offers the following advice to magistrates:

> When you have noted that a particular person has committed contempt of court before you, you should cause that person to be brought before you. You should then frame and record the substance of the charge, read and explain to him, and then ask him to show cause why he should not be convicted on that charge, and give him an opportunity to reply.

His reply should be recorded as fully as possible. You should then decide whether or not to convict him and such decision must also be recorded.

CONTEMPT OF PARLIAMENT

Contempt of parliament may be aptly described as an offence against the authority of the House. As in the case of a Court of Law, when by some act or word any person disobeys or is openly disrespectfully to the authority of the House or wilfully disobeys the lawful commands of the House, that person is subject to being held as having acted in contempt of parliament. Section 24 of the Parliamentary Immunities, Powers and Privileges Act, 1988 (No.3 of 1988) provides as follows:

Any person shall be guilty of an offence (of contempt) who:

a) Having been called upon to give evidence before the Assembly or a Committee thereof, refuses to be sworn or make an affirmation; or

b) Being a witness misconducts himself; or

c) Causes an obstruction or disturbance within the precincts of the Assembly Chamber during a sitting of the Assembly or of a committee thereof; or

d) Shows disrespect in speech or manner towards the Speaker; or

e) Commits any other act of intentional disrespect to or with reference to the proceedings of the Assembly or of a committee of the Assembly, or to any person presiding at such proceedings

We have already seen that the courts are empowered to prosecute, try and punish those who commit the offence of contempt of court, in accordance with the procedure elucidated by Mr Justice Chipeta quoted above. Similarly, one of the corporate privileges of Parliament is the power to punish for contempt of parliament. The procedure for this is normally provided for in the Standing Rules of the House. But in our case, alternative action may be taken against any person who commits the offence of contempt of parliament under the provisions of section 12(3) of the Parliamentary Immunities, Powers and Privileges Act, 1988, which states as follows:

The Assembly or, as the case may be, a committee may, in relation to any act, matter or thing, recommend to the Speaker that he requests the Attorney-General to take steps necessary to bring to trial before a court of competent jurisdiction any person connected with the commission of an offence under this Act.

It is vitally important to underscore the availability of this method of bringing to trial any person who commits an offence under the Act. One of the offences which may be committed under the provisions of that Act, is the offence of perjury. Section 26 of the Act provides as follows:

> Any proceedings before the Assembly or Committee thereof at which any person gives evidence or produces any document, *shall be deemed to be judicial proceedings for the purposes of section (102, 106, 108 and 109 of the Penal Code* (Emphasis added)

Let us take the example of the Parliamentary proceedings of June 24th, 1998; when the House was debating a motion which was earlier moved by Hon Agustine Mrema himself, asking the House to examine and discuss the papers which he had produced before Parliament. According to the above provision, those particular proceedings are deemed to have been judicial proceedings within the meaning of section 102 of the Penal Code; which provides as follows:

> Perjury Cap. 537 102 (1) Any person who, in any judicial proceeding ... knowingly gives false testimony touching on any matter which is material to any question thn depending in that proceeding ... is guilty of the demeanour termed "perjury."
>
> (2) Any person who aids, abates counsels, procures or suborns perjury is guilty of the misdemeanour termed "subornation of perjury."

The punishment for the offence of perjury is provided for in Section 104 thereof, which states as follows:

| Punishment of perjury | 104. | Any person who commits perjury or suborns perjury is liable to imprisonment for seven years. |

Looking back now at that episode with the advantage of hindsight, one could say that Hon Mrema was hugely lucky in the sense that the National Assembly did not recommend to the Speaker that he requests the Attorney-General to take necessary steps to bring Hon. Mrema to trial before a Court of competent jurisdiction for the offence of perjury which the House was satisfied he had committed. A similar conviction by the court would have earned him a handsome seven years jail sentence.

The next transgressor should beware; he/she may not have the same luck!

13

THE POWER OF PARLIAMENT TO
PUNISH A MEMBER

On 24th June. 1998. Parliamentary history was made in Tanzania, when the Member of Parliament for Temeke, Hon. August L. Mrema, was suspended from the service of the House for some 40 days, up to the end of the then budget session.

Because this was the first time ever that such an event had taken place in the Parliament of Tanzania, many questions have been asked about the validity of the action taken by Parliament in this regard. This chapter is intended to explain the powers of parliament in that regard. I have confined my research only to the parliaments of the commonwealth countries. because their rules. practices and procedures are largely identical.

THE PENAL POWERS OF PARLIAMENT IN BRITAIN

It has been authoritatively said that laws are meaningless unless there is power to enforce them by imposing penalties on those who break them. Historically, in addition to relying on the courts, the British Parliament is vested with its own penal jurisdiction. That Parliament has power to punish those who offend it. and the courts do not challenge this power. The House also has the complementary power to define and decide on which actions it may punish. The severest and historically most important power has been that of commitment to prison. The British House of Commons journals show that the House has for many years committed to prison those who challenged its authority, infringed its privileges or otherwise offended against it. In modern times, however, the power of the British House of Commons to commit offenders to prison, although still in existence, has fallen into disuse, the last person to be sent to prison by order of the House was Hon. Mr Bradlaugh in 1880. But its usage survives in a minor form, in that a visitor who misbehaves in the public gallery of that Parliament can be detained until the end of the relevant sitting.

There are two other punishments which can be ordered for members who offend the House. These are (a) expulsion from the House; and (b) suspension from the service of the House for a specified period. Suspension is usually imposed as a mild disciplinary measure. The most recent case of suspension in the British House of Commons occurred on 20th April, 1988, when Mr. Ron Brown, MP., was suspended for 20 days for damaging the mace. But expulsion is the ultimate sanction against a Member. It is an outstanding demonstration of Parliament's power to regulate its own proceedings, and even its composition. It may best be understood more as a means available to the House to rid itself of those it finds unfit for membership, rather than as a mere punishment.

In recent times, British members of parliament have been expelled for perjury, fraud, and corruption. In one particular case, a member was expelled for "conduct unbecoming of an officer and a gentleman." There are some interesting examples. In 1948, Mr. Garry Allighan, M.P., was found to have lied to a Parliamentary Committee. He had wrongly accused fellow M.P.s of accepting money for disclosing to the press proceedings of a private meeting of his parliamentary political party caucus, when that was precisely what he had done himself. The leader of the House moved a motion that Mr. Allighan be suspended for six months without pay. But another member moved an amendment proposing that Mr. Allighan be expelled from the House, instead of being suspended for only six months. The amendment was carried and he was expelled. It is significant to note that Mr. Allighan was a Member of the Labour Party, which at that material time was the ruling party with a huge majority in the House. This shows that on such matters, the British House does not always act on party lines.

THE PENAL POWERS OF PARLIAMENT IN CANADA
In Canada, the right of the Senate and the House of Commons to commit persons to prison for the office of contempt of parliament is regarded as the keystone of parliamentary privilege. Both Houses of the Canadian Parliament have the power to punish their members as well as non-

members for disorderly and disrespectful acts. In other words, the penal jurisdiction of the Canadian Parliament is not confined to its own members alone.

Apart from committing a member to prison, the Canadian House of Commons has power to punish its members also for disorderly conduct and for contempts committed in it while the House is sitting. The punishment can range from reprimand, to suspension, and to expulsion from the House.

The last time a member was so expelled was on 30th January, 1947, when the seat held by Mr Fred Rose, the Member for Montreal, was declared vacant on the orders of the House. Rose had been sentenced to imprisonment for conspiracy to give unauthorised information to the USSR.

EXAMPLES FROM OTHER COMMONWEALTH COUNTRIES

a) Grenada

On 27th August, 1996, the leader of the opposition in the elected House of Representatives of Grenada, Hon. George Brizan, was suspended from the service of the House for a month. That was because of a speech he had made on 9th August, 1996 during the ceremonial state opening of a new session of Parliament by the newly appointed Governor General. In his speech Mr. Brizan raised serious objection to the appointment of the Governor General then in office. Moving a motion for his suspensions, the leader of government business said that "by convention and standing orders, the conduct of Her Majesty the Queen, and that of the Governor - General, who is her representative in Grenada, could not be debated or questioned except upon a substantive motion." The motion considered that these norms had been violated by Mr. Brizan. The motion was carried and Mr. Brizan was accordingly suspended.

b) New South Wales, Australia

On 2nd May, 1996, the Legislative Council of New South Wales in Australia, suspended the Treasurer (Minister of Finance) who was also the leader of the government in the Legislative Council, from the service of the House for the remainder of the day's sitting, because of his failure to comply with an order by the House requiring the tabling of certain papers held by the Government. The suspension of the Treasurer was the culmination of a series of unsuccessful attempts by the Legislative Council to compel the production of papers relating to certain matters of government business which the House wished to discuss. The Treasurer disputed the validity of the resolution for his suspension and refused to leave the Chamber. The Sergeant-at-Arms acting on instructions of the Speaker, quickly presented himself in front of the Treasurer and, without much ado, escorted him from the chamber and out of the precincts of the Parliament.

c) Zambia

The Zambian Parliament still exercises the power of committing persons who offend it to prison. On 30th January, 1996, the Vice President of Zambia, who is the leader of government business in the House, raised a point of order over an article which had appeared the previous day in the *Post Newspaper*, written by one Ms. Lucy Sichone. The Vice-President contended that the said article, which was reporting on a parliamentary debate, was libelous because it had accused him (the Vice President) of fanning violence, when that was actually not the case. The Vice-President also raised another point of order regarding another *Post* article, written by Mr Fred M'membe reporting on the same parliamentary debate. He contended that the two articles were written in a manner which was designed to expose the House to public ridicule and bring down the dignity of Parliament. The Zambian Parliament, by resolution, committed the offending persons to prison and fined them the sum of 1,000 kwacha each.

But there are also reported cases of expulsion and suspension in the Zambian parliament. For example, soon after the two journalists described above were ordered to be committed to prison, one member of Parliament by the name of Hon. Mbikusita Lewanika, wrote a letter to the Speaker, which was first circulated to the press who published it, asserting that the House was grossly unjust in ordering the committal of the journalists. He went on, in very strong language, to dissociate himself from the action taken by the House. Parliament subsequently considered the contents of the letter and the language used therein, and found that the member had "cast gross aspersions on the House and on how it conducted its affairs." He was accordingly charged in a motion before he House, which decided that the assertions by Mr. Mbikusita Lewanika vere derogatory to the dignity of the House; and inconsistent with the standards which Parliament was entitled to expect from its members. It hereupon resolved that he be expelled forthwith from the house for the remainder of the life of that Parliament, i.e. until dissolution. The action created a vacancy, and in accordance with the Electoral Laws of Zambia, the speaker notified the Electoral Commission that a vacancy had occurred in the National Assembly by reason of the expulsion of Mr. Mbikusita Lewanika.

With regard to the suspension of a member, there is the example of one member, Mr. Nalumino Mundia who, on 19th February, 1971, was named for disregarding the authority of the Speaker. The House resolved to suspend Mr. Mundia for a period of three months. He insitituted court proceedings asking the High Court to quash his suspension, but the High Court rejected his application on the ground that according to the Zambian Constitution, internal proceedings of Parliament could not be questioned in any Court.

THE SUSPENSION OF HON. AUGUSTINE MREMA, M.P.

As can be seen from the foregoing discussion, suspension of a member is a power which is legally incidental to any legislature, because it is necessary for any such body to be able to protect its dignity should circumstances warrant. In the Canadian House of Commons, such power to suspend or expel a member is not confined to offences committed by a member during a session of parliament, but extends to all cases where the offence is such, in the judgement of the House itself, as to render the member unfit for parliamentary duties. And as we have seen, British members of parliament have in recent times been expelled for perjury. The Layman's Dictionary of English Law defines perjury as "the willful making of a false statement by someone who has taken the oath as a witness in judicial proceedings." The British experience shows that perjury is an offence also in parliamentary proceedings.

Hon. Augustine Mrema was ordered under the Parliamentary Standing Rule No. 50(2), to produce documents which would substantiate his serious allegations in a speech he delivered in Parliament, that a meeting of government officials had been held on 4th April, 1996, which had decided that three specified persons, including himself, were to be assassinated before the year 2000, and that one of them, retired Gen.

I.H. Kombe, had already been killed as a result of implementing that official scheme of causing death by assassination. He was given five days to produce the necessary documents.

The documents on which he was seeking to rely were duly produced and presented to Parliament on the due date. Parliamentary time was accordingly allocated by the Speaker for a debate to determine whether or not, the documents which he produced had satisfactorily substantiated his allegations of a meeting being held to plan to assassinate him and two others, before the year 2000.

At the end of the debate, Parliament unanimously decided by voice vote, which is the normal method of voting in Parliament, that the documents which he submitted had failed to prove his wild allegations. This is because the document submitted was a statement written by Hon., Mrema himself, claiming that he was told of the alleged meeting of 4th of April, 1996 by the late I.H. Kombe himself, several weeks before he died. The statement claimed that one day in May or June, 1996, the late Kombe had visited Hon. Mrema at his residence and told him the story. The statement claimed further that this was a dying declaration" which had to be trusted. This did not at all convince the House. As far as Parliament was concerned, he had willfully made a wild and serious false statement in the House amounting to perjury. Because he had failed to substantiate that allegation, he had to be punished. A motion was thereupon moved by the Minister of State in the Prime Minister's Office Hon Ngombale Mwiru, for Hon. Mrema's immediate suspension from the service of Parliament for the period ending with the closure of the then budget session.

PARLIAMENT'S JURISDICTION OVER ITS MEMBERS IS ABSOLUTE AND EXCLUSIVE

Since article 100(1) of the Constitution of the United Republic of Tanzania prohibits the questioning of the proceedings of Parliament in any Court or any other place outside Parliament itself, the members participating in its proceedings, such as Hon. Mrema, the M.P. for Temeke, are subject only to the disciplinary powers of the House itself, and cannot appeal to any outside authority. In the Canadian case of *Bradlaugh vs Gossett* (1884) 12QBD 271, when the order of the House to suspend Mr Bradlaugh from the service of the House was challenged in court, it was held that "the jurisdiction of the Houses over their own members, and their right to impose discipline within their walls, is absolute and exclusive."

A Significant Precedent

The decision of Parliament to suspend Hon. Augustine Mrema from the service of the House for a specified period was a very significant precedent. For the first time in its own history, the Tanzanian Parliament exercised its penal powers. The significance of this event lies in the fact that Parliament has now demonstrated its willingness to exercise its powers of punishment whenever it becomes necessary; in order to protect its dignity as a representative of the sovereignty of the people who elected it. In other words, our Parliament has re-affirmed its powers of punishment, which had been dormant for a long period.

But an even more significant aspect of this historical precedent, is that parliament's resolution to suspend Hon. Mrema from the service of the House was adopted unanimously by members of all the political parties which are represented in the House. This shows that, like the British Parliament's resolution described above to expel Mr. Allighan which was uninfluenced by political party considerations; the Tanzania Parliament has also amply demonstrated its capacity to make objective decisions, entirely uninfluenced by political party affiliations.

Consequently, members of parliament of all political parties are advised to take this warning signal seriously, by strictly observing all the relevant rules of the House, as well as the provisions of the Parliamentary Immunities, Powers and Privileges Act (No.3 of 1988). Otherwise the public may well expect to see more such punishments in future. In Hon Mrema's case, it was suspension for a relatively short period. But in future we may as well see the House making use of its other punitive powers of expulsion from the House, or commitment to prison by following the procedure laid down in Act No. 3 of 1988, as the case may be.

Hon. Mrema's Complaints that Parliamentary Procedures Were Violated

At this juncture, it may be best to recall the words of Shakespear in *Troilus and Cressida*, Act III, Scene 2: when Achilles said to Patroclus:

" I see my reputation is at stake,
My fame is shrewdly gored."

Hon. Augustine Mrema has contended in his public statements, that his suspensions for 40 days is invalid because it does not comply with the provisions of Parliamentary Standing Order No. 60(2), which states that for a first offender like him, the suspension should have been for only five days.

But this is a misreading of that Parliamentary Rule. The correct position is that Standing Order No. 60(2) applies only to a member who disregards the authority of the Speaker in such circumstances as are described in Standing Orders Nos. 59 and 60(1). That is when the penalties prescribed in Standing Order No. 60(2) will apply.

However, in the particular case of Hon. Augustine Mrema, there was no question at all of disregarding the authority of the Speaker. On the contrary, he had dutifully done what he was ordered to do, namely to produce before Parliament in not more than five days, documents to prove his allegations of the existence of an assassination plot to kill him and two others, which he claimed had been decided at a meeting of unnamed government officials allegedly held on 4th April, 1996. Hon. Mrema complied totally with that order of the Speaker by producing the documents in the time allocated. For that reason, Standing Order 60(2) is not applicable to him.

Hence, because the penalties prescribed in Standing Order No.60(2) are not applicable to him, Hon. Mrema's case had to be decided on the basis of its own merit, after taking into consideration its particular circumstances. In other words, the Bunge resolution to suspend Hon. Augustine Mrema for some 40 days was made independently of Standing Rules 59 and 60. In this historic case, the Bunge was acting under the authority of the general powers of decision-making which are granted to Parliament by Article 94(2) of the Constitution of the United Republic and Standing Order No. 65(1) of the Parliamentary Rules. It did not act in excess of its powers as some people seem to believe.

In the second place, Hon. Augustine Mrema has contended that the action taken against him is invalid because the provisions of Standing Order 50(2) were violated, in the sense that he should have been interrupted at the time when he made his allegations and asked to substantiate them. He asserts that requiring him to substantiate those allegations long after he had finished his speech, as was done by the Prime Minister, was a violation of Standing Order 50(2)

That clearly is a literal interpretation of Standing Order 50(2). But this literal approach to statutory interpretation was rendered obsolete years ago in a judgement of the English Court of Appeal, in *Northman vs Barnet London Borough Council* (1978) All ER 1243, where Lord Denning, M.R. said:

> The literal method (of construction) is now completely out of date. It has been replaced by ... the purposive approach. In all cases now in the interpretation of statute, we adopt such construction as will promote the general legislative purpose underlying the provision.

Therefore when, as Speaker, I concurred with the Prime Minister's request and ordered Hon. Mrema to produce before the House the documents which would substantiate his allegations, I was applying the purposive approach in interpreting Standing Order No. 50(2). I was, and still am, of the opinion that the legislative purpose underlying Standing Order 50(2), was to prohibit members of parliament from willfully making false allegations, in other words, from telling lies in Parliament. Because if they are allowed to do so and get away with it, serious damage will be caused to the reputation and dignity of the Parliament. Hence, failure to require Hon. Mrema to substantiate such serious allegations as he had made in his speech, for the reason only that he had not been interrupted at the time when he was actually speaking, would surely be a serious failure in the duty to promote the remedy which was intended in order to suppress the relevant mischief. I believe that such failure would have given rise to an absurd and totally unjust situation.

In any case, such interruption would have made no difference to his plight, other than making it worse! What actually happened is that he was given three separate opportunities to prove his case, namely:

a) Five days to produce the necessary documents;
b) Enough time to speak in support of his documents, not limited to the normal maximum of 15 minutes parliamentary speaking time;
c) The right to reply at the end of the debate, which was again suspended from the 15 minutes.

Yet, after fully utilising all these opportunities he still failed, in the opinion of the House; to substantiate his allegations. Requiring him to do so immediately by interrupting his original speech would surely have made matters even worse for him. Could it be possible perhaps, that Hon. Mrema's current complaints are only a true reflection of Shakespeare's words quoted above?

> "I see my reputation at stake,
> my fame is shrewdly gored"

REFERENCE

The following is the text of the various Parliamentary Standing Rules which are quoted in this article:

S.0. 50(2) A Member when speaking in the House on any motion, is required to ensure that all what he says is strictly accurate and factual; does not contain allegations, inferences or imputations, or based on hypothetical cases. The Speaker, or any other Member rising on a point of order, may make a demand on the Member who is speaking to substantiate his Statement.

If he refuses to do so, he shall be regarded as having violated the provisions of Standing Order No. 59.

S.0.59(1) The Speaker, after having called the attention of the House to the conduct of a Member who persists in irrelevance or tedious repetition, either of his own arguments or of other Members in the relevant debate, any direct the Member to discontinue his speech and resume his seat.

(2) The Speaker, may order a Member to withdraw immediately from the House for the remainder of the sitting; and may direct such steps to be taken as are required to enforce his order.

S.0.60(1) Where a Member disregards the authority of the Speaker by refusing to comply at once with the order to withdraw from the House, or persistently and willfully obstructs the business of the House; the Speaker may name such Member for disregarding the authority of the chair. Whereupon the following steps shall immediately be taken against the offending Member.

S.0.60(2)(a) Any other Member may move a motion that offending Member be suspended from the service of the House. The Speaker shall put the motion to the vote, no amendment, adjournment or debate being allowed.

14

"PUBLIC HEARING" AS PART OF THE
PARLIAMENTARY LEGISLATIVE PROCESS

INTRODUCTION

During the passage of the Bill for the 13th Amendment to the Constitution of the United Republic through its various parliamentary stages in January/February. 2000. various experts were invited to Dodoma to express their views before the Parliamentary Legal and Constitutional Affairs Committee on the merits and contents of the said Bill. Although this is a well established procedure in many Commonwealth parliaments, yet its fairly obvious benefits had still to be meticulously explained to some members of our parliament. including some Government ministers, in order for them to fully appreciate its inherent value.

The purpose of this chapter is to explain to the general reading public about the benefits of this particular procedure. as part of the on-going parliamentary civic education programme. Essentially, this particular procedure is intended to provide an opening for direct public participation in the work of their parliament: with specific emphasis on people's participation in the law-making process.

THE LAW-MAKING PROCESS

A major function of any parliament is the making of laws. In fact, the terms "parliament" and "legislature" (i.e. the body that legislates) are often used synonymously. In parliamentary language. a draft law is referred to as a bill. A bill can be an original piece of legislation. or it can be a proposal to amend or repeal an existing law.

Under the rules of procedure of the Tanzania Parliament, a bill can be introduced in the House either by the government, or by an individual member of parliament. But traditionally, it is the government which has always played the dominant role in initiating legislation. This is in fact the case in most Commonwealth countries which continue to operate the Westminster parliamentary system. In the British House of Commons itself, a limited amount of time is usually made available for business introduced by back-benchers, i.e. members who are not ministers or do not hold any other government office. But bills which are presented by such members very rarely reach the statute book.

This is because the demand from back-benchers to introduce private members bills is so high that ballots have to be held regularly to determine the members whose bills will be brought before the House for debate, and successful members usually consider themselves very lucky to have obtained a debating opportunity.

Under Tanzanian parliamentary procedure, all bills, whether they are government or private members' bills, must pass through a compulsory stage of consideration by an appropriate standing committee, before they can be introduced into Parliament for formal discussion.

"PUBLIC HEARING" AT THE COMMITTEE STAGE

"Public hearing" is a procedure whereby any parliamentary committee which is considering a bill, i.e. the draft of a proposed law, invites interested members of the public to give their opinions on the contents of the relevant bill. The basic principle underlying this procedure is the principle of peoples' participation in the law-making process.

Under this procedure, witnesses are called to give evidence before the committee which is considering a particular bill. These would normally be experts or persons who have an interest in the subject matter of the proposed legislation.

The Merits of the Procedure

The legal draftsmen of a bill usually have to consider not only its legal and technical aspects; but consideration must also be given to its political consequences, should it eventually become part of the law of the land. Each new bill has legal consequences in the sense that it must be consistent with both the constitution and the existing legislation. But in addition to the legal nature of a bill, many items of legislation also have technical consequences, and the advice of expert witnesses may be very useful in that regard. Furthermore, many bills also have political consequences, in the sense that they affect various sections of the community in one way or another. Hence in many countries, persons or groups interested in or affected by an item of legislation, are routinely given the opportunity to express their interest at an appropriate stage of the legislative process. In many parliaments, such consultations are held at the committee stage of the consideration of a bill. For example, in the House of Representatives of Australia, standing committees may hear evidence from interested persons or groups. But generally speaking, provisions have been made for experts to be invited to present evidence before a standing committee of the House in many of the Commonwealth parliaments, including Canada, Cyprus, India, Malaysia, New Zealand, and the United Kingdom. Experience in these parliaments has shown that this procedure helps to speed up the bill's passage through parliament, by reducing opposition to it because of amendments which are usually made as a result of such consultations.

THE ESSENTIAL ROLE OF PARLIAMENTARY COMMITTEES

Parliamentary committees have been described as "the most effective vehicles for making parliaments more responsive, representative and relevant." This is basically due to the fact that parliamentary committees normally operate on a non-partisan basis, i.e. free from the strict party discipline which is normally applicable in parliament itself.

Because they meet in camera, parliamentary committees are freed from the constraints of observing party lines. Hence the points of agreement can be readily identified; while legitimate differences of opinion can be expressed in less adversarial terms. This therefore ensures a rational examination of issues and all viable alternatives. It also enables the committees to be more constructive in developing solutions to the problems facing the society which they represent in parliament.

However, it is important to emphasise that parliamentary committees must not only listen to lobbyists, or pressure groups, or the articulate organised minorities alone; they have a responsibility also to listen to interested ordinary citizens who may wish to express their views before the relevant committees, and provision must be made to enable this to happen.

PUBLIC HEARING TO BE INCORPORATED IN THE RULES OF THE HOUSE

As a result of the favourable reception of the public hearing procedure by most members of our parliament and ministers, recommendations have already been made to the Standing Rules Committee of Parliament for the procedure to be incorporated in the rules of the House.

This procedure was initially tried out on two previous occasions during the year 1999. The first occasion was when the Bill for imposing severer punishment to persons found guilty of sexual offences was being considered by the relevant committee of parliament. The second occasion was when another parliamentary committee was considering the Land Bill and the Village Land Bill. On both occasions there was a high approval rating for that new procedure which at that stage was being used on trial basis.

Because the same high approval rating has also been scored when the procedure was applied to the recent 13th Constitutional Amendment Bill, it is now proposed that this should become a permanent feature of our law-making process. Members of the Tanzanian public are therefore invited to prepare themselves for active participation in our law-making process by making full use of this new participatory process.

However, because of the cost factor involved; the Speaker will have to exercise caution in authorising the use of this procedure, so that initially, it will be applicable only to few selected bills which are of great public interest or importance.

15

THE CCM PARLIAMENTARY BACK-BENCH REBELLION OF NOVEMBER 1998

INTRODUCTION

The following quotation is taken from a book entitled *"Members of Parliament: The Job of a Back-bencher"* published by the Macmillan Press Ltd. in 1990:

> In the days immediately following a general election, the Palace of Westminster is full of earnest men and women. They are the new members of the new (British) Parliament; and for many the job to which they have just been elected is a bit of mystery.

Here in Tanzania, most of the procedures which are followed by the country's Parliament have always remained "a bit of a mystery" to members of the media and the public at large. That is probably the reason why a recent parliamentary event of great significance with regard to the extent of the practice of democracy within parliament itself, passed almost unnoticed by the Tanzania public. I am referring here to the historic event which occurred in the House during its session in November 1998 and which, in the language of parliament, is known as a "back-bench rebellion." This was a great event signifying the presence of a healthy environment for democratic record for future reference. What actually happened is that on that day, for the first time ever in the history of the House, the government actually lost in a free vote on a motion moved by back-bench member of the ruling party, CCM.

THE FACTS OF THE CASE

The facts surrounding this event were as follows: On 3rd October, 1998 the government published in the official Gazette, a bill whose short title was given as "The Government Pensions Act, 1998" and was scheduled to come into operation on 1st July, 1999. The bill was to be submitted to the National Assembly for consideration at its November, 1998 session. The rules of that august House require that any proposal which is to be considered by the National Assembly must first be referred by the Speaker to a relevant committee for detailed scrutiny. The appropriate relevant committee in this case was the Constitutional and Legal Affairs Committee, which is chaired by Hon. Arcado Ntagazwa, MP. (CCM). The Bill faced early difficulties in its passage through the Committee, particularly with regard to one of its clauses, which sought to raise the retirement age for the public service from the current 55 years to 60 years. But the government seemingly failed to take proper notice of these early warnings, and took it for granted that there would eventually be no problem, even after a meeting of the ruling party caucus had expressed similar reservations about this particular provision. Apparently relying on its huge majority in Parliament, the government believed that it could propel the bill's passage through all the procedural stages in the House without difficulty.

The *laissez-faire* attitude displayed by the government on that occasion can be compared and contrasted with the much more accommodating and positive attitude taken by the British Labour government chief Whip in 1963, when he said:

> If a minister were to say to the Cabinet that 'if you introduce this legislation, there is likely to be a great deal of opposition from our own back benchers,' I am pretty sure the cabinet would think twice about introducing that particular legislation which would be likely to cause trouble for them on the floor of the House.

In our own case, the voices of dissent by a large section of the CCM back-benchers were ignored, the government went ahead and carried the bill through its second reading stage. But the more crucial stage was still to come, namely the committee of the whole house, where each clause of the bill is considered individually and passed or rejected, as the case may be. The disputed clause was clause No. 17 (1) and (II), which read as follows:

17 (1) The age of voluntary retirement from service shall be fifty years.

(2) Subject to section 16(e), an officer who attains the age of fifty years may at any time opt to retire but an officer who does not opt to retire, shall continue in office in the service on pensionable terms until he attains the age of sixty years which is the age of compulsory retirement.

With intent to try and challenge the government on this provision, a CCM back-bench member of parliament, Hon Parseko Vincent Kone, MP for Simanjiro, filed a notice of a motion to be moved at the said committee stage seeking to delete from the relevant clause of the bill the words "sixty years" and substitute therefor the words "fifty-five years." The effect of the amendment would be to reject the proposal of sixty years as the age of compulsory retirement and retain the current fifty-five years. His notice was duly accepted by the Speaker and circulated on the material day to all members as part of the day's Order Paper.

During the deliberations of the committee of the whole House, when clause 17 was called for consideration, Hon. Kone dutifully rose in his place in order to catch the chairman's eye. On being recognised by the chair, he quickly moved his motion for amending the said clause.

As was of course to be expected, when the motion was put to the vote, it was vehemently opposed by the government front benches. But the majority of the CCM back-benchers, who were joined in this particular activity by the opposition benches, voted strongly in support of Hon. Kone's motion. It was therefore easily carried. So the government lost. This is the historic back-bench rebellion of November 1998. History had indeed been made; and a precedent had been established. Hopefully too, a usefull lesson had been learnt.

A WHOLLY LEGITIMATE PARLIAMENTARY ACTIVITY

Back-bench rebellions of this nature are perfectly legitimate parliamentary activities in multi-party parliaments, and they normally occur whenever the government fails to listen to the voices of dissent within the ranks of its own back-benchers. There are several examples of this back-bench activism in the records relating to the British House of Commons, both when the Conservative Party was in power as well as when the Labour Party was in power, some of which are reproduced below:

a) In 1963/64, the ruling Conservative Party introduced a "Resale Price Maintenance" Bill. The records say that the Bill met with intense opposition from within the Conservative Party. Almost fifty of their members abstained or voted against the government on the second reading of the Bill.

b) In 1981 a "Fuel Tax" was introduced. A threatened revolt by Conservative back-benchers forced the Chancellor of the Exchequer to halve the proposed increase in the tax on diesel fuel withdrawn.

c) On the introduction of new immigration rules in 1983, the Home Secretary conceded to persistent opposition from his own party members regarding a restriction of the right of entry to husbands of British citizen women, whereby husbands would have to prove that the marriage was not just to beat the immigration rules.

There are also examples of similar events occurring when the Labour Party was in power:

a) In the debate on the proposals for the reform of industrial relations in March 1969, fifty-five Labour MPs voted against the government, and another forty Labour members were estimated to have abstained deliberately.

b) In a vote on the "Queen's Income" in February 1975, almost ninety Labour MPs voted against the government's proposal to increase substantially the queen's income from the government.

Hence, the CCM back-bench rebellion which occurred in November 1998 in the Parliament of Tanzania should not be seen as unusual or uncalled for. The availability of this strategy is extremely helpful in that it creates the need for a functional partnership or alliance between the government and its back-benchers, and greatly improves the work of parliament generally. If the government gets to know that its proposals are likely to be rejected by its party's own back-bench members, it will certainly exercise much greater care in the preparation of those proposals, in order to make them acceptable. This is what makes the said event one of substantial historic importance. For, it helps to correct the widely held but erroneous view, that the back-bench members of the ruling party are rendered ineffective because of the strict party discipline which supposedly requires them to always speak and vote only in support of their government's proposals. The event which is described in this chapter shows clearly that the position of the back-benchers of the ruling party is in fact very different. As was clearly demonstrated on that occasion, the ruling party back-bencher still has the freedom to criticise the government and even to vote against it, without necessarily attracting any disciplinary action.

16

THE ROLE OF PARLIAMENTARIANS IN FIGHTING AGAINST CORRUPTION IN TANZANIA*

THE MEANING OF CORRUPTION

What does the word "corruption" precisely mean? Most people who talk about corruption tend to equate corruption with bribery. But in actual fact, corruption is a much wider term, of which bribery is only a part.

In the public service area, corruption includes wrongful deviation from the basics which are laid down in the relevant laws, rules or regulations governing a particular branch of the public service. In the political field, corruption also means decomposition of the political system. This is because politics is about governance. Politics is a commitment to a mission; and it is a kind of trust or faith. Corruption is what degenerates a political system into misgovernance, lost commitment, forgotten mission; betrayed trust and broken faith. That, I wish to submit, is the type of corruption we should be talking about.

THE FIGHT AGAINST BRIBERY

But we must at the same time fully address the question of bribery as a menacing ingredient of corruption in Tanzania. As shown on the seminar programme, there will be a sharing of experiences from Kenya, Uganda and Tanzania, with regard to the efforts being made to curb corruption in our respective jurisdictions. In the case of Tanzania, those Hon. members present here who belong to the ruling party (CCM) will readily recall the relevant provision of the Party Constitution which spells out

---

*Originally delivered to a judges' seminar by the author in Dar es Salaam on 19th January, 2000

clearly that "Bribery is the enemy of justice," and enjoins each party member to promise on oath that he or she will never give or receive bribes. This particular provision has been in existence right from the time of its predecessor (TANU). But it appears to have had no impact on the behaviour of party members. How can this deficiency be remedied?

THE ANTI-CORRUPTION LEGAL REGIME

On 22nd April, 1971, the Parliament of the United Republic of Tanzania enacted the Prevention of Corruption Act (No. 6 of 1971), which defined the full range of "corrupt transactions" and imposed severe penalties on those who would be found guilty of an offence under that Act. In 1974 this law was amended to enable the President to establish an anti-corruption body. Yet this measure too, appears to have had little impact in curbing corruption in the country, as is evidenced by the report of the recent Warioba Commission on Corruption, which makes the following comment in its report:

> There has been a large increase in our country of people who demand bribes and those who give bribes. The nation has also witnessed an increase in the use of state power for personal gains among public servants. At the same time, incidents of non-observance of the laws of the land have also greatly increased ...

Why has this law been largely ineffective in combating corruption?

CORRUPTION IN THE POLITICAL FIELD

An important ingredient of corruption in politics is what may be termed as "electoral corruption." This is so because corruption in the electoral process is primarily responsible for political corruption among the elected leadership.

The celebrated historian Edward Gibbon (1737-1794) described corruption in his classical work entitled *The Decline and Fall of the Roman Empire*, as "the most infallible symptom of constitutional liberty." His statement has been interpreted in the context of individual liberty, to mean that freedom of the individual includes the freedom to be corrupt.

In an excellent book about corruption in India published in 1995, entitled *Politics of Corruption*, the author contends that one of the biggest sources of direct electoral corruption in that country, was the collection of funds for political parties, ostensibly for financing what is described as "party work;" whereas in fact, the lien between the party chest and the personal pocket was totally obliterated. The author refers in particular to the amendment which was made by the Indian Parliament to their Companies Act, in order to forbid companies from contributing to political parties. What is of particular relevance to the discussion, is the corruption loophole which was (perhaps inadvertently) created by this move. The author's comments on that issue are as follows:

> If companies were allowed to make donations to political parties, they would be obliged to disclose it to the shareholders and their accounts would be statutorily audited. But once such open donations were banned by law, there was no limit to unaccounted for or secret donations being made to all and sundry who had access to the centers of power, in exchange for a quid pro quo. It became free for all in terms of fund collection. No one knew from who and for whom. Everyone in a position to do so, merrily went about that job without any accountability.

Here in Tanzania a number of election petitions which have been brought to court over the years, have included allegations of electoral corruption. One example arising out of the 1980 one-party elections, is the case of William Bakari and another *v* Chediel Yohane Mgonja (Civil appeal no. 5 of 1982). In that case, the counsel for the petitioners included in his pleadings an allegation of corrupt practices by the first respondent *Chediel Yohane Mgonja*. Another example arising out of the multi-party elections held in 1995 is the case of Dr. Medard Mutalemwa Mutungi *v* Sebastian Rukiza Kinyondo (1998). Dr. Mutungi, the losing candidate petitioned the High Court seeking to void the election on a number of grounds, one of which was corruption by the winning candidate. There are numerous other examples of allegations of corrupt practices in every round of elections. It is clear therefore that the question of electoral corruption in Tanzania is very real and needs to be addressed. How can this menace be effectively dealt with?

WAY OUT OR ENDLESS TUNNEL?
I want to strongly suggest, that the focus of public discussions should be on finding a viable solution to the problem of corruption. It is a point of great significance that corruption is punishable by law, in the same

way as any other offence. In other words, corruption is a crime in every sense of the word. The existence of corruption is roundly condemned by our society, and is widely considered to be an unmitigated evil. Corruption is also proscribed by a law which provides for severe punishment for a variety of corrupt acts. And yet, corruption continues to prosper in this country. Why?

It appears that any amount of brain-racking and mind-wrenching about a way out of this problem always ends up in frustrating futility. People talk about it casually almost every day with everyone who has anything to say about it, lamenting that it is impinging upon the day to day life of our citizens. Everyone waxes eloquently on the evils of corruption, but as soon as it comes to the point of visualising or suggesting a way out, everybody tends to run out of ideas; and quickly resorts to saying that "the government must do something about it."

The government of course has an obligation to do something about it, since corruption is a crime. But there are two ways of dealing with a crime. One is to wait until the crime is committed, its victims to go and complain to the police; then latter to nab the suspected criminals, put them on trial, and get them punished by a Court of Law. The other way is to prevent the criminals from committing the crime, or catch them in the act so that they do not succeed. Most people will agree that the second course is far better in the interest of society as a whole. In both respects, however, both the government and the general public have a shared responsibility, with regard to prevention of corruption. There is one possible way in which legal remedy can be applied to handle the situation. This involves the plugging of loop-holes in our laws and regulations, in order to prevent corruption. The identification of such loop-holes is precisely the task which was given to the Warioba Commission which I referred to earlier. But since the Warioba report was published, no legislative proposals have been introduced so far in parliament for the purpose of plugging the identified loopholes. Why?

CONCLUSION

I wish to conclude by saying the following: Corruption is like a virus which is always around to infect a political system anywhere in the world, and make it sick. In Italy, a Socialist Party official was arrested in Milan in 1992, having been caught pocketing a bribe on a cleaning contract in an old people's home. This ostensibly minor event set in motion an anti-corruption avalanche which quickly swept away Italy's veteran political leaders. In Japan, former Prime Minister, Noburu Takeshita, was forced to resign in 1989 after a recruit shares-for-favour scandal exposure. That proved to be the beginning of the end of the Liberal Democratic Party as the most powerful political outfit in Japan. The world is spacious enough to enable anyone to cite many more instances. But let me return to my virus theory.

If this virus is allowed its full play without any resistance or check, it will eat into the vitals of the system and eventually destroy it. But very much like the human body, political systems are capable of developing their own immune systems which can automatically fight and resist the virus. The degree of corruption prevailing in any one political society depends on the strength or deficiency of its immune system. In a democratic polity, a strong and vigilant public opinion is the built-in immune system which resists and restricts the onslaught of viruses like corruption.

Hence my considered view of the role of parliamentarians in fighting against corruption, is that because they are the elected representatives of the people, the parliamentarians' most important function is to act as public opinion-leaders in their various areas of responsibility, in order to create a strong and sustainable public opinion which will resist the onslaught of the virus of corruption. For, as Edmund Burke (1729-1797) is reported to have said, "for evil to triumph, it is necessary only for the good man to do nothing." Therefore let each parliamentarian be the 'good man" who does something to curb corruption in his area of jurisdiction.

PART TWO

17

THE SEPARATE ROLES OF PARLIAMENT AND THE JUDICIARY*

I am always willing to engage in constructive dialogue with the press. I wish therefore to comment on your editorial of 13-19 March, 1998, which poses the question "who will police the police, investigate the investigators?"

The answer is simple: The courts. The Courts of Law have a very crucial role to play in any society, the Tanzanian society included. That role is to deal with every person who is suspected of breaking the law. It means that any person who causes the death of another person commits an offence and must promptly be arraigned and brought before a Court of Law. It makes no difference whether the person who commits the offence is a policemen or a *"jambazi."*

Mr Editor, you may not have had a chance to study Administrative Law, and may consequently be unaware of the powers which are given to the courts to exercise judicial control over any administrative excesses perpetrated by public authorities. The basic rule is that a public authority (including of course the police): may not act outside the powers granted to it by law (the doctrine of *ultra vires*). If that happens, the courts are empowered to take appropriate remedial action. That is why the answer to your question of who will bell "the police cat" must emphantically be: the courts: and certainly not parliament or any of its committees!

---

* Dialogue With *The Family Mirror Newspaper*

Parliament played its proper role when it enacted the Police Force Ordinance (Cap. 322 of the Laws of Tanzania). This law prescribes in sufficient detail the powers of the police force and how they are to be exercised. Hence, if certain members of that force happen to indulge in acts of violence which are not mandated by the said law, they will be acting in excess of their legal powers, and are therefore subject to judicial control.

Mr Editor, you probably did not see the actual petition by the 21 MPs which they submitted to the Speaker. The import of that petition was to the effect that such police killings constitute a violation of Section 14 of the country's Constitution, which guarantees the right of every person to life; and that the taking away of that life by a policeman is therefore a violation of that section of the Constitution. Hence their request that the matter should be investigated by the relevant Parliamentary Standing Committee, which is empowered to investigate such suspected violations of the Constitution. But what about the other person's life, which is also brutally taken away by a *jambazi?* Are there two categories of killings: one category being that which violates the Constitution (to be dealt with by Parliament); and a separate category of killings, e.g. by *jambazis,* which does not constitute such violation (to be dealt with by the Courts?)

Mr Editor, like any other citizen, you are of course entitled to hold and freely express your opinions, as you rightly did in your editorial. But unfortunately your opinions appear to be based on the lack of a proper understanding of the underlying constitutional principles relating to the separation of powers and functions between the Legislature's power and the Courts.

18

THE SEPARATE ROLES OF PARLIAMENT AND THE JUDICIARY*

Dear Mr Editor, I was greatly amazed by the editorial in issue No.026 of he *African* newspaper. dated Tuesday, March 10, 1998. The heading of hat editorial was: "Speaker must not tramp police agenda," and went on to assert that "dismissing such important social agenda on mere echnicality is. therefore. not the best approach for the Speaker." I am amazed because my ruling in that matter was not based on "mere echnicality." It was based on the provisions of the Laws of Parliament tself. i.e. the Standing Orders of the House, which must always govern he transaction of any of its business. I am amazed because Mr. editor seems to treat this parliamentary law as "mere technicality." Therefore wish to borrow his own words and respond as follows: **Mr Editor, you should not tramp on the rules of parliament!**

I explained clearly in my ruling. that Parliament has no power to discuss any matter which is before a Court of law. That provision is a fundamental principle of constitutional law which deals with the profound doctrine of the separation of powers between the Legislature and the Courts; and should never be regarded as "mere technicality." as the said editorial seems to imply. Because this was one of the main reasons why he MPs request was rejected. his accusation that "Msekwa does not suggest any other options for the legislators to pursue the matter" is

---

* Dialogue with *The African Newspaper*

entirely misconceived. This is so because there is just no other option for the legislators, so long as cases arising out of what is termed as "Police brutality" are before the courts. Hence, his suggestion that one option for the legislators is to table a private member's motion is in fact no option at all; because the same rule which forbids parliamentary discussion of matters which are before the courts will also be applied to such a motion. That is precisely the point which Mr. Editor of *the African* seems to have sadly missed.

Furthermore, that editorial talks about the need for Parliament "to redefine the role of the Police Force." The legislature s position with regard to that particular aspect is that the role of the Police Force is adequately defined in the Police Force Ordinance, Cap. 322 of the Laws of Tanzania. Any policeman or woman who violates the provisions of that Ordinance commits an offence. (not a breach of the Constitution). Hence, he must be dealt with according to the law which is relevant to that offence. And that is actually what has been happening in all the cases which the group of 21 MPs wanted to investigate. Does it really require an expensive parliamentary investigation to establish that simple fact? My answer was NO; and I believe I was right.

Finally, I would like to make it clear that my rejection of the now famous request by a group of 21 MPs, was not based on a technicality. It was a result of a proper application of the rules of the House. The Speaker is always bound to be guided by the rules of the House in the performance of his functions. That is what guarantees his impartiality, which is so crucial for the proper and efficient functioning of any parliament, especially a multi-party parliament. If ever a day will come when the Speaker will allow himself to be influenced by popularity considerations, to the extent of ignoring the rules of the House in order to gain some cheap personal popularity with particular groups of MPs; that will be a sad day indeed for the institution of parliament. My constant prayer therefore, shall be that it should not happen during my speakership.

19

INTERVIEW WITH ROBERT MIHAYO OF
BUSINESS TIMES - 26TH MAY, 1997

Q.1 Virtually all the major political parties in Tanzania, including the ruling party are now embroiled in varying levels of turmoil. What do you think might be the reason for this? Is this the natural outcome of multiparty politics? What does this augur for multi-partism in Tanzania?

ANS. I am answering this question in my capacity as a political scientist only, and not as Speaker of the National Assembly; because the question of turmoil in political parties has nothing to do with parliamentary business.

As a political scientist, I disagree with your statement that "virtually all the major political parties in Tanzania, including the ruling party, are now embroiled in varying levels of turmoil." Certainly there is no turmoil within the ruling party; and there is no evidence of turmoil in the rest of the political parties either, except the NCCR-Mageuzi. That being the case, it cannot be said that it is "a natural outcome of multiparty politics" as you put it. It is rather a result of internal problems which are specific to a particular political party; and such problems can always be solved amicably, within the affected party itself, by using the said party's constitution and procedures for solving internal problems. Multi-partism is here to stay. It will not be derailed by such periodic internal conflicts within individual political parties. These are temporary problems which can be overcome without affecting the functioning of multi-partism itself as a viable political system.

Q.2 You have recently taken a keen interest in sensitising college and secondary school students about the constitution. Why have you developed this interest at this particular point in time?

ANS. The only reason for my keen interest is the recent introduction of multi-party politics in Tanzania. Previous to that, the leading political institution in the country was the ruling party. Hence the activities of the ruling party were matters of great importance to all the people. But with the change to multi-partism, Bunge has now become the leading political institution in the country. Hence the activities of Bunge have assumed great importance to all the people. Bunge is one important section of the country's constitution. Therefore learning about the functions of Bunge is at the same time part of learning the Constitution itself. It is infact better for the students to learn the Constitution as a whole, instead of learning only one section of it, namely Bunge. That is why my office has introduced this programme of public civic education concerning Bunge, plus the Constitution as a whole.

Q.3 While many people appreciate your efforts in sensitising students about the constitution, some observers doubt whether the Speaker is the best person to undertake this task. They say the office of the Speaker does not have the required manpower and infrastructure to undertake this task successfully. Moreover they don't understand the rationale for leaving other youths and adults out of this programme. What do you say?

ANS. The Speaker has only undertaken the preliminary task of sensitizing the public about the importance of understanding the Constitution. The intention is to integrate all this material into the formal education system of our country; both at the school education level and the adult education level. When the relevant teaching or reference materials have been assembled and approved by the Ministry of

Education authorities, especially the curriculum developers, the job of teaching will be taken over by the large number of civic education teachers who are already teaching this subject in our schools and colleges all over the country. It is of course true that the Speaker's office does not have the manpower to undertake this mammoth task. The Speaker has only taken the initiative of inaugurating the programme. Its continuation will depend entirely on the regular teachers of civics education. I believe that the noble principle of peoples' participation in the affairs of their country can only be successfully applied if the people themselves are made aware of their constitutional rights, duties and responsibilities. This awareness can only be created by helping them to understand the contents of the Constitution. Hence the crucial importance of this civic education programme, and the urgent need for its continuation in schools and adult education centres.

Q. 4. During the G55 MPs campaign for a three tier structure of the United Republic of Tanzania you endorsed the proposed three governments structure. However, after Mwalimu Nyerere subsequently intervened and argued for the retention of the two government structure, you changed your position and sided with him. In your book on the transition to multi-partyism you supported the opposition demand for a review of the constitution. However you have recently been reported as being opposed to such changes in the constitution. This has prompted some critics to accuse you of being "shifty" and "inconsistent." Could you comment on this?

ANS. But you are surely aware that I issued an immediate denial of those inaccurate media reports which wrongly said that I am opposed to changes being made in the Constitution. That was a misrepresentation of fact by one reporter who obviously had not understood my message. I therefore wish to repeat here, with appropriate emphasis, that I am not and cannot possibly be opposed to changes being made in the Constitution, because I believe that a viable Constitution is not a static document. It should be flexible enough to be able to accommodate desirable socio-political changes.

I therefore stand firmly by what I stated in my book on the Transition to Multi-partyism as follows:

I believe the need for a new Constitution, which will take into account the new multi-party political situation, is quite obvious and cannot honestly be disputed. What appears to be in dispute is the *methodology* of obtaining the views of the people of Tanzania concerning the contents of the proposed new Constitution.

Georges Bidault once said that "the good or bad fortune of a nation depends on three factors: Its constitution, the way that constitution is made to work, and the respect it inspires." Obviously, a rigid constitution which does not allow for change cannot inspire confidence.

Therefore my friendly advice to all those people who mistakenly think that I am "shifty" or "inconsistent," is that they should read and believe only what I have written myself in this respect. They should completely disregard what was misrepresented by some mischievous journalist as being my statements, when in fact I did not say any such thing!

For purposes of putting the record straight, I wish to repeat here what I actually said when I was misreported. My statement was that the general public should be given an opportunity to understand the contents of our country's Constitution before involving them in the process of changing it. It is such understanding which will enable them to become active participants in the process of changing the Constitution, for then they will be making informed decisions and choices about what should or should not remain in the Constitution.

As you can see, this is very different from saying that I am opposed to changes being made in the Constitution!

What I am campaigning for is an informed public which can discuss the Constitution more profitably.

Q.5 Multi-partism is being accused of having the ironical effect of stifling free expression by MPs in the National Assembly as they are now bound by party discipline to support the positions of their respective parties. Could you comment on this charge.

ANS. This may indeed be so in those parliaments where the ruling party has only a tiny majority. But in our National Assembly, where the ruling party has such a huge majority, the party sees no need at all to apply the party whip on its MPs. And indeed, because of its huge majority in Parliament, CCM has so far not yet found it necessary to bind its members of parliament not to criticise the proposals which are put forward by the CCM government. Your readers may wish to know that the parliamentary whipping system is done in a special form, which is a written direction from the Chief Whip to all MPs of his party, instructing them what to do in a particular case. But since the beginning of the multi-party Bunge, this has not been done. Therefore CCM members, and I believe the opposition members as well, have been largely free to speak and vote as they. The speaker's office new programme of parliamentary civic education will help to clarify this matter in greater detail.

But for the time being let me just explain the basic principle which is involved, namely the principle of adherence to the party's election manifesto. In all multi-party electoral competitions, candidates are expected to conduct their election campaigns on the basis of their party's election manifestos. The election manifesto is a written document containing a list of promises which a given political party makes to the voters, with a clear commitment that if that party is elected to office and forms the government, it will use its governmental authority and resources to implement those promises. The election manifesto is therefore binding upon the said party. Any political party which wins the election and forms the government becomes morally bound to implement its election promises which are contained in its election manifesto. Consequently, the issues which are presented to Parliament by the government of the ruling party are intended to implement those election promises. Therefore, the MPs of that party are also morally bound to support the passage through Parliament of all such issues.

Thus, it is misleading to talk about "free expression in the National Assembly by MPs," because they are not free to disregard the promises which they made to voters during their election campaigns. For if they do so they will be committing a moral offence of cheating the people for political gain, by making false promises. Hence the importance of party discipline and the party whip; whose sole purpose and function is to ensure that their MPs will adhere faithfully to their party's election promises.

Q.6 Opinion appears to be divided on what is the suitable electoral system for Tanzania. Some people feel that the present 'winner-takes-all' system should continue because it is not only simple but also familiar. Yet others feel that it should be replaced because it is excessively costly as it frequently requires voters to go back to the polls for by elections. They suggest that an alternative electoral system which is less costly to taxpayers is called for. What is your position on this issue?

ANS. My firm opinion is that, this is a matter of immense public importance, which should be widely discussed in order to reach agreement on what is the most advantageous electoral system in our circumstances. Obviously, both systems have their strengths and weaknesses. It is mostly a question of choosing which of these is more appropriate for a country like ours.

My own assessment is that a mixture of the two systems, as in the Federal Republic of Germany, is the most ideal choice for Tanzania. I have already organised a seminar for members of the Parliamentary Constitutional and Legal Affairs Committee which will take place during the first week of June, i.e. next month. The pros and cons of the proportional representation electoral system is one of the subjects to be discussed at that seminar. I believe PORIS, a non-governmental organisation, is also organising a special seminar which will have a much wider participation by members of the public on the same topic. It is clear therefore that serious discussion will be taking place on this matter in the near future. So let us wait for the outcome of those discussions.

Q.7 An increasing number of Tanzanians, probably including voters from your own constituency, are complaining that the government's tight fiscal and monetary measures are making life miserable for them. As an MP what would you like to tell your voters and the government about this matter.

ANS. Patients who seek medical treatment are sometimes obliged to accept bitter medicines in order to get a cure for their illnesses. I personally believe that the tight fiscal and monetary policies of the government are a necessary prescription for curing the economic illnesses of our nation. As an elected M.P., it is both my duty and responsibility to explain this to my constituents, and I have done so regularly in my public meetings in my constituency. No democratically elected government anywhere in the world would deliberately adopt policies which are detrimental to its people. Such policies. which in the short term appear to be harsh, are normally adopted only as a means to an end which will be beneficial to the majority of the people in the longer term. I personally support that kind of approach, because I believe it is good management policy.

Q.8 Many would-be investors have criticised Tanzania's legal regime for investment as being not investor-friendly. Since legislation is the domain of the National Assembly, is the House not betraying the interests of the nation by passing such hostile legislation? What efforts is it taking to undo the harm done so far?

ANS. It is difficult for me to comment on that allegation that the legal regime is not investor-friendly, because no particulars have been given of the non-friendliness of the relevant law in that regard. What I can say is that Parliament has the sovereign authority not only for making laws, but also for unmaking them. If it is shown on a motion moved in the House. that a certain piece of existing legislation does not achieve the purpose for which it was intended. Parliament will quickly change it or even repeal it.

But a motion must be moved in the House itself for that purpose. Such motion can be moved by any private member, upon satisfying the requirements of the relevant standing rules of the House. That is the only way in which Parliament can positively intervene in such a matter. because that is the *modus operandi* of all parliamentary Institutions. So, does any of our M.P.s wish to take up this challenge?

Q.9 What has been the most challenging moment to you in your career as Speaker of the National Assembly? How did you cope with that challenge?

ANS. Whenever the Speaker is actually sitting in the Chair of the House, every single moment is challenging. As I pointed out in my book entitled "Essays on the Transition to Multi-partism in Tanzania," the main function of the Speaker is to preside over meetings of the

House in full session and in Committees of the whole House. This is a quasi-judicial task which can be fulfilled satisfactorily only by strict observance of the doctrine of impartiality. In this respect, the Speaker can be compared to a referee in charge of a game, who is obliged to see that it proceeds smoothly and according to the rules.

In presiding over the meetings of the House, the Speaker has many sensitive tasks to perform. His basic task is to ensure that debate continues in an orderly manner. Hence, should the House, for example appear to be getting a little out of hand, he must control the situation quickly by calling for order. Any failure to respond to his authority by the House as a whole may lead to the adjournment or suspension of its sitting. In a situation where an individual M.P. makes a remark which is out of order, he will be asked by the Speaker to withdraw that remark and apologise.

Should the member refuse to do so, he will be immediately "named," i.e. charged, for disrespect to the authority of the chair, and this may lead to his temporary exclusion from the House for a specified period. Thanks to God, so far during my tenure of office as Speaker, I have not had to cope with any of the sensitive situations described above. But the mere fact that something of that kind *could* happen without prior notice, remains a constant reminder for the Speaker to be alert and attentive at all times, so that should it really happen, he will be able to deal with it effectively and efficiently.

20

1 You have been in the media of late discussing, in particular, the 1998 Constitutional White Paper. In my opinion, what you have said has positively fanned the debate, but in the process you have been attacked personally. Do you still have some steam to defend the proposed White Paper approach? How have you taken the attacks against you on this issue?

NS. I am not aware of any personal attacks on this issue. But who in his right senses would want to attack me personally? The issue to be discussed is whether the government White Paper is an acceptable method of involving the people in discussing Constitutional amendments. Every person is entitled to express his/her opinions. That is everyone's constitutional right. Attacking me for expressing my views is, to say the least, very primitive. It may be opportune once again to remind such persons that simple minds discuss persons, ordinary minds discuss events, great minds discuss ideas. Anyone who attacks me personally, instead of discussing the concrete issue of the White Paper, clearly belongs to the group of those with simple minds.

I hope one day they will advance themselves to the civilised stage of discussing issues, rather than persons. This is because everyone is constitutionally entitled to express his/her views and opinions. If cogently. The public will then make their own judgement as to which views to accept.

Q.2 But some people think you are saying what you are saying not out of knowledge and conviction, but because you are a CCM member, interested in ensuring your political survival. Are they wrong?

ANS. Those who are saying so should know that in the first place, I am a CCM member out of conviction. Therefore, naturally, I support CCM also out of conviction. A member of any political party is expected to support its policies. I would like to believe that all those who left CCM and joined opposition political parties did so out of conviction!

Hence I am proud to be a member of CCM because I am convinced that it has the right policies, which I also support. So what I said regarding the white paper is based on personal knowledge of the history of government White Papers in this country. If anyone has any evidence to the contrary, let him produce that evidence.

Q. 3 Tanzania has a very young population. Do you usually have this in mind when you present your arguments?

ANS. A young population does not obliterate history. English judges continue to apply court precedents which were established more than a century ago. In other words, in the conduct of public affairs, it is always useful to do some research into the past, to see if a helpful precedent can be found which can be applied to the instant case. That is why I quoted the 1962 and 1982 White Papers, in order to disprove the claim that the white paper approach is restrictive. I am sure the young generation also profits from this knowledge of history. But I have an additional personal reason which explains my own love for history. It is because I studied history for my first degree course at Makerere. I have continued to appreciate the value of history to this day. This is the true reason for my historical approach in discussing the relevant public issues, such as the white paper issue.

Q.4. Some people in the opposition parties argue strongly in favour of a national constitutional conference, something you are known to oppose. Why do you oppose the conference? But why do you really disfavour the national constitutional conference, an approach we are told has produced good results beyond Tanzania's borders? Some people think the proposed conference is something popular with the electorate. Do you have different views? Some people argue that the conference promotes democracy than the white paper approach. What are your views?

ANS. My own personal views concerning the national constitutional conference issue were clearly expressed long ago in 1995, in my book which was published by the Dar es Salaam University Press early that year. At page 108 I stated as follows:

> Some political parties have expressed the view that a constitutional Conference should be convened, consisting of representatives from all the fully registered political parties, as well as from civic groups and other interested organisations; and that it is such a conference which should decide on what should go into the constitution. I would like to argue against the suggestion of a constitutional conference.
>
> My objection is based primarily on the democratic principle of the *mandate*, namely, that any group of persons seeking to speak or decide on behalf of the people, must have a clear mandate from the people concerned. Such mandate can only be obtained by means of free and fair elections which are held specifically for that purpose. A conference which consists only of hand picked delegates who are not elected by the people, would obviously have no mandate to decide on behalf of the people. Hence the undesirability of giving such an important constitutional task to a conference consisting entirely of nominated or even self-appointed delegates.

That is still my stand even to day, which is four years later so I have nothing to add. I believe this answers all the supplementary questions accompanying your main question.

Q.5 The Secretary General of Chama cha Demokrasia na Maendeleo (CHADEMA), Mr. Bob Makani, was on Tuesday quoted as saying that white paper proponents are tragically demonstrating their ignorance of the existing fundamental law. Is he somewhat right? He was quoted as drawing your attention to article 8 of the

Constitution of the United Republic of Tanzania, showing you and people who share your views, that you are wrong in favouring the white paper approach. What is your comment?

ANS. Mr. Bob Makani, like myself and everybody else, is entitled to his opinions. That is one of his constitutional rights which must be respected. Whether he is right or wrong is for the public to judge, my point is that we should allow everyone to express his/her views uninterrupted by attacks: and let the public decide which views to accept.

Q. 6 You have said that you strongly believe that the white paper approach is a good methodology, but opponents think the government will do "something" to restrict public discussion of its proposals. Do you still have some defence?

ANS. I believe that my case is well articulated in my article which was published by the *Daily News*. My plea is that we should not cross the bridge before we reach it. Let the white paper be published first, and let the government tell us the procedure for discussing its proposals which will be contained therein. If the procedure turns out to be restrictive, we will know at that time. In my published article, I pointed out that discussion on the previous white papers was not restricted, and that it is reasonable to expect that the government will be bound by its own precedents. At least that is my personal opinion, and I claim my constitutional right of expressing that opinion.

Q.7 Suppose the government became unwilling to accept proposals outside the white paper?

ANS. My answer is the same: do not cross the bridge before you reach it. You are asking what will happen if the government became unwilling to accept proposals outside the White Paper. I think I am entitled to ask: What makes you think that the government will do so? History shows that with regard to past white papers, the government was willing to accept some proposals which were made outside the white papers. What is your evidence for assuming that the contrary will happen this time? Let us please avoid speculation, and wait for the facts to come out.

21

Q.1 The 31ˢᵗ Commonwealth Heads of Government meeting opened in Edinburgh on Friday. Is this meeting generally an important meeting for CPA?

ANS. The Commonwealth Heads of Government bi-annual meeting is an event which is completely separate from, and unconnected with, the Commonwealth Parliamentary Association. The Heads of Government meetings are serviced by the Commonwealth secretariat, which is headed by H.E. Chief Emeka Anyauko as its Secretary General; while the CPA is serviced by a different secretariat headed by its own Secretary General, Mr Arthur Donahoe, Q.C. The CPA concentrates mainly on parliamentary issues of common interest among Commonwealth parliamentarians, while the Heads of Government meetings deal with more substantive matters of policy such as good governance and economic co-operation within the Commonwealth. This means that the two bodies are operating at two different levels. For that reason, the Heads of Government meetings have no direct bearing on CPA as such.

Q.2 Has it been an important summit for CPA (Africa Region) historically?

ANS. No.

Q.3 On the whole, does the CPA normally expect 'something' from all or most of the summits?

ANS. No.

Q.4 Am I right to suggest that you handed over the chairmanship of the African Region Speaker's Conference in May this year; where and during what occasion?

ANS. That is quite correct. The chairmanship of the CPA Africa Region Speaker's Conference rotates among the speakers of the member parliaments on a two year basis. Therefore in May 1997, my term of office came to an end, and the Speaker of the Seychelles Parliament, Hon. Francis MacGregor, M.P., was elected as chairman of our group for the next two years. The election of the new chairman was held at the end of this year's bi-annual conference which was held at the White Sands Hotel, Dar es Salaam, during the last week of May, 1997.

Q.5. What new office have you assumed in your association (CPA)?

ANS. Last year, at the Annual CPA Conference which was held in Kuala Lumpur, Malaysia, in August 1996, I was elected to the Executive Committee of the International CPA. I will be serving in that capacity for a period of three years, at the end of which somebody else from the CPA Africa Region will be elected to take my place. Representation to the International Executive Committee is on the basis of representing the C.P.A. regions.

Q.6 Chief Anyaoku talks of the principle of democracy to which all member countries, must subscribe and must be seen to practice. But at International level democracy seems to have more than one colour: Meaning this to one group and another thing to another group. Is this part of the harsh realities of the post-cold war world?

ANS. At the Commonwealth level, there are certain central features of democracy which are accepted uniformly by all its members, and this really has nothing to do with the post cold-war situation. These features were in existence even during the cold-war period, and they remained intact at the end of that period. The relevant central features are the following:

a) Government by elected representatives of the people;
b) The holding of regular periodic free and fair elections for the election of those representatives;
c) Good governance; which involves:
   i) Transparency in-decision-making;
   ii) Respect for human rights;
   iii) Strict adherence to the principles of the rule of law and in particular, adherence to the provisions of the county's constitution.

To a every large extent, these features are to be found in all the systems of government of what are known as democratic countries, both in the Commonwealth and outside it. There are of course certain variations of one kind or another, which have been necessitated by the need to adjust the system to suit local conditions in individual countries. For example, whereas in almost all the democratic countries, electoral competition is based on competition between political parties: the people of Uganda under the leadership of President Museveni, have recently adopted a different system altogether, which is a "no party" system.

Q.7 Some leaders have accused the West of imposing a western type of democracy on poor Southern countries. What is your views on this?

ANS. The claim that Western countries have "imposed their Western type democracy on the poor countries of the South must surely be false; and probably comes from autocratic leaders who would like to rule their nations like tribal chiefs. If a poor country of the South adopts something from the rich countries of the North, that does not necessarily mean that what they adopted has been "imposed" on them. For example, most of the countries of the South have adopted the educational systems of the North, and in most cases adapted it to suit their individual local circumstances. That surely can not properly be called an "imposition!" Similarly, most of our countries have adopted Western democratic systems of government, and adapted them to suit their individual local situations. I believe this is not, and should not be described as an imposition. The central features of a democratic system which I have already described can be found in all truly democratic countries, but with certain slight variations to suit the local conditions of particular countries.

Q.8 You are also the Speaker of the National Assembly; are you satisfied that Tanzania subscribes to the principle of democracy and, in your opinion, is this country increasingly seen to practice this important Commonwealth principle?

ANS. Yes, as Speaker of the National Assembly, one of my functions is to preside over the development and maintenance of the democratic culture in the House. In that respect, I am completely satisfied that after taking-off properly with the election of a multi-party parliament in October 1995; we have continued to lay the necessary firm foundations for its maintenance and durability. I actually have heard many people commenting that so far multi-partysm is working properly only inside Parliament; but it is not doing so well in the rest of the country as a whole. I am personally inclined to concur with these views.

Q.9 Nigeria's Commonwealth membership is currently suspended. What has the CPA (Africa Region) done to help Nigeria get a democratically elected government? How about Sierra Leone?

ANS. The only possible option which is available to CPA with regard to member countries who depart from the accepted Commonwealth democratic norms is to kick them out of the association, and leave them out there in the cold until they themselves decide to return to the democratic way of life. Nigeria was kicked out of CPA long ago; and Sierra Leone was also kicked out in May this year, as a result of the military coup which took place there. The CPA has no mandate to help any country to get a democratically elected government. That is entirely the business of the country concerned. The CPA will only welcome them back into its fraternity as soon as democracy is restored in that country's system of government.

Q.10 Do you (CPA-Africa Region) ever help the Commonwealth Ministerial Action Group when it comes to issues related to Africa?

ANS. No. The Commonwealth Ministerial Action Group is an organ of the Commonwealth Heads of States and Governments. And as I said earlier, that body is completely different from CPA. Because that group was created by the Heads of States and Governments, it draws its support from the Commonwealth member governments; and not from the C.P.A.

Q.11. Chief Anyaoku also talked about respect for human rights in Commonwealth countries. Do you think the CPA is happy with the general performance of Commonwealth members on this issue?

ANS. Whether CPA is happy or unhappy is really immaterial. What is important is that the CPA does allocate time in its annual conferences, for a discussion of this important subject; primarily in order to keep it sharply in focus; so that Commonwealth legislators are constantly reminded of their significant role in protecting human rights through appropriate legislation in their own individual countries.

Q.12 Tanzania is, I hope, an important CPA member. Yet in Tanzania, especially in Zanzibar, some voices say loudly that Tanzania is not doing well in this score. What is your comment? (Tanzania in general and Zanzibar in particular?)

ANS. In Tanzania, the basic legal rights are spelled out clearly in the Constitution of the United Republic, 1977. Any contravention of them is therefore actionable in any court of law which has competent jurisdiction. Therefore, the best and most reliable evidence of contravention of human rights should be the number of actions which are brought before the courts in order to seek appropriate remedy. I am not aware of any such actions having been brought before the courts so far. Hence, it may be that the "loud voices" which you may have heard could well be from people who are more concerned with politics than with speaking the whole truth and nothing but the truth!

Q.13 The Commonwealth wants to see Tanzania subscribing and be her best in this regard; Do you have illustrative examples?

ANS. I think the position is clear enough for anyone who wants to see to be able to do so. The "rule of law" is defined in the *Layman's Dictionary of English Law,* as "the principle that all citizens of a country are subject to the same laws; and that no one can be punished for something not expressed to be illegal." I have seen no evidence which shows that the contrary is the case here in Tanzania. But the term "rule of law" has a number of other meanings too. Its primary meaning is that everything must be done according to law. Viewed in relation to governmental functions, the rule of law doctrine requires that every government agency must base all its actions on the authority of the law, so that any person who might be adversely affected by any action by the government or any of its agencies, can seek redress in the courts. Our courts have the power to invalidate the said action if it is found to be inconsistent with the law or to be a misuse of the powers granted to it by law.

All these provisions and remedies are available in Tanzania's legal system.

Q.14 Is Tanzania doing her best to maintain or achieve good governance? Would you wish to say something about the constitution in relation to this question; something Tanzania should ponder over?

ANS. Maintenance of the rule of law which we discussed in the preceding question is part of good governance. Conducting the affairs of the nation in accordance with the provisions of the constitution is extremely good governance. Furthermore, accountability of the government leaders, and transparency in the decision-making process, are also essential elements of good governance. Tanzania does not of course have an abundance of these qualities in its system of government: but they are not entirely lacking either. I would like to draw a lesson from the following quotation:

> He that goeth about to persuade a multitude, that they are not so well governed as they ought to be, shall never want attentive and favourable hearers. Richard Hooker C.1554-1600.

As I have no intention of looking for "attentive and favourable hearers," I am able to say confidently that there is a large measure of good governance here in Tanzania.

But I must sadly add that there are few elements in our community, who are deliberately trying to disturb the rule of law, purely for their own political ends. As I said earlier, conducting the affairs of the nation in accordance with the provisions of the Constitution is what constitutes good governance. Section 98 of the Constitution of the United Republic of Tanzania, 1977, sets out very clearly, the procedure to be followed for amending that constitution. But currently there are efforts being made by certain individuals and groups in our society, to try and circumvent that constitutional process by advocating and calling for amendments to be made to our country's constitution through a process which is not in conformity with that which is provided by the Constitution itself. Namely, they want to convene what they call an all party "Constitutional Conference."

I have said this before, and I will say it again here very loudly, that such a conference has *no mandate* to decide on any constitutional changes. The democratic principle of the mandate is well established in all representative democracies. It means that any group of persons seeking to speak or decide on behalf of the people, must have a clear mandate given to them by the people concerned. Such mandate can only be obtained by means of free and fair elections which are held for that specific purpose. A conference which consists of hand-picked or self-appointed delegates who are not elected by the people themselves for that particular purpose, will *definitely* have no mandate to decide on constitutional provisions on behalf of the people.

Professor Emanuel Nabuguru of Makerere University Kampala, once said at a seminar in Arusha in 1993 which I attended, that "years of political chaos in Uganda had bred a group of Ugandans who thrived on unconstitutionality and disorder." I wish to recommend that all Tanzanians of good will should act decisively together in order to prevent, by all lawful means, the emergence of a similar group of people here in Tanzania, who seem to want to thrive on unconstitutionality and disorder; thereby creating a fundamental breach of the cherished principles of the rule of law.

I may even caution here that since the function of amending the constitution of our country is a privileged and exclusive function of the Parliament of the United Republic, therefore any person or group of persons who might be tempted to illegally usurp that function, will be summoned to appear before the Powers and Privileges Standing Committee of Parliament, in order to answer charges of attempting to usurp the lawful powers of Parliament in law making.

22

INTERVIEW WITH *THE SUNDAY NEWS* -
11TH OCTOBER, 1996

Q.1 You are the chairman of the Commonwealth African Regional Parliamentary Association. Is this correct and how do you get the chairman of the region?

ANS. The Commonwealth Parliamentary Association (Africa region) operates at two levels, namely:
a) The Regional Parliamentary Conference, and
b) The Regional Speakers' Conference.

The established system in our association is that of a rotating chairmanship, each chairman assumes responsibility for one year, that is to say, from one annual conference to the next following annual conference. So I was indeed chairman of the African Regional Conference of the Commonwealth Parliamentary Association for the year ending in March 1996, when I handed over the chairmanship to the Speaker of Lesotho.

I am now the current chairman of the African Region Speakers' Conference, which again is a rotating chairmanship, but this one rotates on a two-year basis. I assumed this particular responsibility in June 1995, and will be handing over to the next chairman in May 1997.

Q.2 How often does the Commonwealth African Regional Parliamentary

ANS. The Regional Parliamentary Conference meets annually in a different member country: but the Speakers' Conference meets annually. also in a different member country.

Q.3 How would you summarise the objectives of the Commonwealth Parliamentary Association (CPA)?

ANS. The following are the stated objectives of the Commonwealth Parliamentary Association:

The purpose of the Association is to promote knowledge and education about the constitutional. legislative, economic, social and cultural systems within a parliamentary democratic framework: with particular reference to the countries of the Commonwealth of Nations: and to other countries having close historical or parliamentary associations with it. The association pursues these stated aims:

a) By arranging annual Commonwealth Parliamentary Conferences in different member countries:

b) By arranging study groups, meetings. and seminars which may be on a local. regional or commonwealth-wide basis:

c) By organising international visits to enable parliamentarians to exchange views and to inform themselves on matters of common interests;

d) By the publication of journals, monographs, pamphlets, reports of conferences. and seminars, and other papers relevant to the aims of the association.

Q.4 Do you have something you call the official policy of the CPA?

ANS. Yes. the official policy of the CPA is the strengthening of parliamentary systems: and the promotion of the democratic principles of good governance. transparency and the rule of law in the member countries of the association.

Q.5 Your association is said to have a patron and a president? Who is the present patron and president? What are the duties of each?

ANS. Yes, in each member country of the association, the Head of State is ex-officio patron of the local branch of the association, and the President of the local Branch is the Speaker of the Parliament of the country concerned.

Q.6 Who are the CPA members and what are the membership conditions?

ANS. Membership of the Commonwealth Parliamentary Association is open to all persons who are for the time being members of parliament of the country concerned. But former members of parliament are also eligible to join as associate members. But membership of the internal CPA is accorded only to the parliaments of member countries; and not to individual MPs.

Q.7 Your explanation seems to suggest that membership is accorded to the legislature of a Commonwealth country. What happens when the military overthrows an elected government?

ANS. In every case where the military overthrows an elected government, in any member country, the membership of that country is automatically suspended, and the local branch remains in abeyance until the country concerned reintroduces democratically elected parliament and government: whereupon it may apply for readmission to membership of the CPA.

The decision to re-admit a country whose membership was in abeyance is taken by the Annual International Conference of the CPA, upon recommendation by its executive committee. A recent example in our region was the re-admission in August this year, of Uganda into membership of the CPA. Uganda was suspended in 1971 when Iddi Amin overthrew the elected government of that country.

Q.8 The cold war influenced things in all countries. Great changes have taken place since its end. Has the end of the cold war been of any significance to your association?

ANS. There are no visible signs of our association having been influenced by the end of the cold war. This is because our association is based primarily on relationship which were established during the days of the British Empire, which subsequently (after decolonisation) became the Commonwealth. These relationships were themselves based on similarities of parliamentary practices and procedures, and the common use of the English language. These factors had very little, if anything, to do with the cold war. That is why the termination of the cold war has had no visible influence on our association.

Q.9 Have you set. or in your opinion, what should CPA's priorities be in the post-cold war period?

ANS. There is no reason whatsoever for expecting any change of CPA priorities in the post-cold war period. The associations' objectives remain unchanged. and its priorities also will remain unchanged.

Q.10 How does a Commonwealth citizen benefit from the existence of the CPA?

ANS. The CPA is designed to benefit only its members, and not the ordinary citizen. This is because the association is not a government of any kind. It is a body which brings together parliamentarians for the purpose of exchanging views and experiences in the performance of their duties as the elected representatives of their people. The association offers no direct services to the ordinary citizen.

Q.11 What does the Commonwealth African Regional Speakers' Conference do and who are its members?

ANS. As stated earlier, the Commonwealth Africa Region Speakers' Conference is a gathering of the parliamentary speakers of the countries of the Commonwealth which are situated in Africa, including the Island nations of Mauritius and the Seychelles. The Speakers' Conference is convened once in every two years, for the purpose of enabling speakers to exchange views and experiences regarding parliamentary procedure and practice in their respective parliaments.

Q.12 When did the Speakers last meet and when are you meeting again?

ANS. The Speakers' Conference of the Africa Region Commonwealth Parliamentary Association was last held in Lilongwe. Malawi, in June 1995, and the next meeting will be held here in Tanzania in May 1997. Those conferences are normally held in the country of its chairman. I am the current chairman, so the next conferences is coming to Tanzania.

23

INTERVIEW WITH *THE BUSINESS TIMES* -
13TH JANUARY, 1996

Q.1 What special attributes are required to lead a multi-party Legislature as compared to a single party one? Does this apply to Tanzania?

ANS. The most important attribute of the speaker of any multi-party parliament is impartiality in the execution of his/her duties. He/she is expected to guide and control the debates inside parliament without fear or favour. He/she has to give a completely objective interpretation of parliamentary rules and to ensure strict adherence to the practice and procedures of the House. It is essential that all members of the House, irrespective of party allegiance, are accorded their due parliamentary rights by the Speaker.

The person who is elected to the office of speaker of a multi-party parliament has to bring to it the utmost integrity, persuasive ability, and erudition. Not only must the Speaker be impartial, he must also appear to all sections of the House, and to the nation, as a whole, that he/she is impartial in his/she conducting of the business of the House. These attributes clearly also apply to the new multi-party parliament of Tanzania.

A speaker who is also an elected member of parliament like myself, has to operate two sets of relationships; firstly with his/her fellow members of parliaments, and secondly with his/her political party. With regard to the first, he/she must show that he understands the psychology of his/her fellow members in order to earn their respect and their regard. In other words, he/she must be sensitive to the mood of the House. He/she must act wisely and firmly, preferably with a sense of humour when tempers are on edge. While dealing with members of the House, the speaker cannot afford to discriminate between those belonging to the ruling party and those of the opposition. He/she has to inspire members with a confidence about his/her sincere efforts to give correct rulings, uninfluenced by passion or prejudice; and unswayed by their impact on his/her personal position.

With regard to the speaker's relationship with his/her political party, it must be remembered that the speaker gets elected to the House on the ticket given to him/her by his/her party. Hence he/she is not in a position to completely severe his/her connection with his/her party, as he/she has to get the party ticket again when he/she seeks re-election. For example, I have just returned from a Commonwealth Speaker's Conference in Cyprus, and there we were told by our host, the Speaker of the Cyprus Parliament, that he/she is the vice-president of his/her political party, the Cyprus Democratic Party. However, this relationship should not in anyway affect the impartiality of the speaker in guiding the proceedings of the House, which he is required to do strictly in accordance with the procedural rules which are established by the House itself. It is only through the effective application of those rules, plus the prudent exercise of his/her discretion; and by establishing his/her own credibility as an impartial umpire in the House, can the Speaker win over and retain the confidence of members of parliament as well as that of the general public.

Q.2 It is sometimes claimed that Tanzanian voters can only vote their representatives (member of parliaments) into the National Assembly, but it is very difficult, if at all possible, for them to recall those MPs, if these representatives fail to meet the voters' expectations.

Apart from using the party, or unless the MP contravenes the law or the constitution, are there any other constitutional provisions that would enable voters to recall their representative for failing to do his/her job?

ANS. Apart from the exceptions which you have mentioned, there are no other legal or constitutional provisions which would enable voters to recall their elected representative.

But I must explain further that the provisions that voters can only vote their representatives into parliament but cannot recall them if they fail to meet the voters' expectations is to be found not only here in Tanzania, but also in the majority of the countries of the world. The published results of a study which was conducted in 1976 by the *International Center for Parliamentary Documentation* in 168 countries show that only 18 of those countries had made provision for the recall of a member by his/her electors if he/she betrays their confidence. Among them were: Hungary, Bulgaria; China; Congo; Cuba; Czsechoslovakia; Democratic Republic of Yemen, German Democratic Republic; Malawi; Mongolia; Poland; Romania; USSR; Yogoslavia; and Indonesia. In all the remaining countries, their members of parliament could not have their mandates revoked by the electorate. Tanzania belongs to that majority of countries which have no provision for the electorate to recall their members of parliament.

Q.3 You have just returned from a trip to Cyprus, what was the purpose of your trip?

ANS. I went to Cyprus to attend a regular Conference of the Commonwealth Parliamentary Speakers. These conferences are held every two years in a different country of the Commonwealth, and the Cyprus meeting was the 13th in the series. This was my second conference to attend, the first one was in January 1994 in Papua New Guinea, when I was Deputy Speaker carrying out the duties of the then Speaker Chief Adam Sapi, who, for health reasons, could not travel to that meeting.

Q.4 It is understood that Tanzania is later this year playing host to a Commonwealth Parliamentary Association meeting. What exactly will be the purpose of this meeting and why is it being held in Tanzania?

ANS. We are not holding any meeting of the Commonwealth Parliamentary Association in Tanzania this year (1966). We indeed held a meeting last year (1995) of the Africa Region of the Commonwealth Parliamentary Association in Arusha. That meeting was held in Tanzania because I am the current chairman of the Africa Region of the Commonwealth Parliamentary Association, which brings together 14 parliaments of the African countries which are members of the Commonwealth. Again this was a regular meeting of that group, which meets every year in a different African Commonwealth country, in order to compare notes and exchange experiences in the field of parliamentary practice and procedures. The 1996 conference will be held in the Kingdom of Lesotho.

Q.5 In your view, are there any opportunities which Tanzania as a host country might use in furthering the growth of democratic rule and the rule of law in our country?

ANS. As I have already indicated in my answer to the preeceeding question, the main purpose of these parliamentary conferences is to exchange views and experiences, with the objective of making desirable improvements in the conduct of parliamentary business in our individual parliaments, for the general enhancement of democratic rule and effectiveness.

Q.6 What do you see as the future of democratic rule and the rule of law in Tanzania?

ANS. I think the future is very bright. I am of the firm view that in any democratic country, the institution of parliament is the custodian of democracy and the rule of law. It is for that reason that I and my parliamentary staff are determined to build and strengthen our newly elected multi-party parliament so as to enable it to effectively play its role as the custodian of democracy and the rule of law in Tanzania.

Parliamentary democracy as a system of governance is in essence also a mechanism for the protection of human rights. For human rights are a matter of domestic law and practice, and all laws require the approval or validation of parliament.

Furthermore, the executive, or the Government, is accountable to Parliament. Therefore Parliament is the only institution through which the sovereign will of the people can be effectively expressed. Parliament is therefore in a very unique position which gives it a clear mandate to safeguard the people's democratic aspirations and interests, and the rule of law. Our parliament already has effective in-built mechanisms and procedures for carrying out this important function. These include provisions for the passage of bills into laws: for amending the constitution; for the ratification of international conventions which are entered into by the government: for the enforcement of government's accountability to parliament through its committees; and through various other channels which are available to members of parliament to raise matters of public concern through questions and motions presented to the House.

Q.7 There was, and remains, a general feeling particularly within the opposition, that the Constitution of the United Republic is full of patches and only caters for the interests of a single party in the era of multi-partism.
   a)   What are your views on this?
   b)   Do you think this had any adverse effects on last year's general election?

ANS. Yes I am aware of that general feeling, because the issue of the constitution has been raised on several occasions by the opposition parties. My own views, which I have already expressed in my recent book entitled *"The Transition to Multi-partysim in Tanzania,"* are as follows:

   a)   No constitution can be permanently static. A viable and sustainable constitution must be sufficiently flexible, so that it can be amended in order to accommodate changing circumstances as and when they occur. With the advent of mutlipatysim in Tanzania, I personally believe that the country needs a new constitution which will take into account the changed political situation. That was also the unanimous recommendation of the Nyalali Commission, of which I was a member.

b) However, I do not accept the view that our present Constitution is "full of patches" and caters only for the interests of a single Party, and that it had adverse effects on last years' general election. The constitution is a country's basic law. Its primary objective is to lay down the Executive, the Legislative and the Judicial institutions of the country concerned; to describe the functions of each of those institutions; and to provide for the distribution of powers among them. The Constitution of the United Republic was also designed to achieve the above objectives. And since 1992, Parliament has made several amendments to the constitution, in order to facilitate the proper functioning of the country's new multi-party political system. If these amendments are what some people mistakenly call "patches," then they should understand that all constitutions in the world do get amended from time to time. Because it is the only legal method of bringing the constitution up-to-date.

c) With regard to the allegation that the constitution had adverse effects on last year's general election, I would like to point out that elections are governed not by the constitution as such, but by an entirely different law, which is the Elections Act (No.1 of 1985). as amended up to July, 1995. The Elections Act was extensively amended in order to ensure that it was fair to all the parties. Direct evidence of this fairness can be seen by looking at the numerous election petitions which have been filed. The main complaint in all these petitions is not that the constitution itself, or the election law, was unfair; but rather that the provisions of that law were not complied with. Therefore the constitution cannot be said to have had any adverse effects on those elections, and the fairness of the Elections Law is not being challenged either.

Q.8. The Nyalali Commission recommended, *inter-alia*, that the 40 laws it said were oppressive or had been overtaken by events, be repealed. The phase II Government under retired President Mwinyi turned a deaf ear to the recommendations, what chance does the recommendation stand under the new Parliament?

ANS. It is certainly not true that the phase II Government under retired President Ali Hassan, Mwinyi turned a deaf ear to the Nyalali Commission recommendation regarding the 40 specified laws. I am a member of the Law Reform Commission of Tanzania; and I can confirm that the 24 Laws which were recommended for repeal or review, and which are the responsibility of the Union Parliament (the remainder are Zanzibar laws and are therefore the responsibility of the Zanzibar Government and House of Representatives) were formally referred to the Law Reform Commission, which has already prepared a preliminary position paper on each of the said laws. That paper is entitled "Position Paper on the Laws Identified in the Nyalali Commission Report."

The Law Reform Commission is currently continuing with its professional examination of those laws. It should be possible for the Commission to submit its final report in the near future, so that the Union Government and Parliament can take appropriate action.

Q.9 The Tanganyika agenda in the National Assembly and the related proposal for establishing three governments will almost certainly feature in the coming session of the National Assembly.

It is said that you were pro-Tanganyika. and that may be that is why Mwalimu Nyerere did not support your candidacy for the Presidency.

a)   Is it true that you favoured the Tanganyika motion in the National Assembly?

b)   Does that explain why Mwalimu did not support you in your presidential aspirations?

c)   If the answer to (a) and (b) are in the affirmative, have you now changed or do you still maintain your stand?

ANS. I have not yet been notified by any Member of Parliament, as is required by the Parliamentary rules of procedure, of his/her intention to introduce the Tanganyika agenda in the forthcoming session of the National Assembly. What I know for certain is that such a proposal cannot be submitted by any CCM member of parliament. The reason for this apparent restriction is adherence to Party discpline. In a referendum in which all members of CCM were invited to participate in 1995, the majority vote was in favour of retaining the two-government structure of the Union, thus rejecting outright the proposal for the establishment of a Tanganyika Government within the Union. That NEC resolution is binding to all CCM members, including CCM members of parliament. It should be remembered that soon after that CCM NEC resolution was adopted in August, 1994, the National Assembly itself voted to withdraw its own resolution which it had passed earlier calling for the establishment of a Tanganyika Government within the Union. At the time the National Assembly consisted entirely of CCM members, who took that action in a show of obedience to their party's policy directive. Therefore it will be a serious breach of party discipline for any CCM member of parliament to re-introduce that subject. Now to answer your specific questions:

a) It is indeed true that I personally favoured the Tanganyika motion when it was introduced in the National Assembly in August 1993. That was completely in line with my earlier position in the Nyalali Commission Report, wherein I appended my signature in support of the proposal for the establishment of a Tanganyika government within the union structure.

b) It is completely untrue to say that Mwalimu did not support my candidature for the Presidency. The truth is that all those who were not supported by Mwalimu Nyerere were left out of the short-list of six names which were submitted to the National Executive Committee of CCM. My name was on that short list, which shows that Mwalimu did not oppose my candidature. In any case, I had myself stated publicly at a press conference, that should Mwalimu Nyerere oppose my candidature I would immediately withdraw. He did not oppose my candidature and therefore I did not withdraw.

c) The answer to the question whether I have changed my position or I still maintain my stand is that, as I have already explained, I am a CCM member and therefore I am bound by the CCM resolution of August, 1994, which re-affirmed the party's policy of a two-government structure of the Union. You may be interested to know that Mwalimu Nyerere himself was in favour of one government only for the Union, i.e. without a Tanganyika government or a Zanzibar government. But he too, being a CCM member, is bound by the CCM policy of two-governments. So if you are looking for a loser in this particular issue of changing the union government structure, both Mwalimu Nyerere and I are losers!!

24

INTERVIEW WITH *THE BUSINESS TIMES* -
11TH DECEMBER, 1996

Q.1 What do you consider to be the major achievements of the first multi-party Parliament during its first year of existence?

ANS. In order to correctly quantify the achievements of Parliament in any given period. I believe it is necessary first of all to have a clear understanding of what parliament's functions are; so that the achievements can then be assessed by looking at parliament's performance of those functions during the specified period. The main functions of our parliament are:

a) To enact the laws of the country:

b) To provide. by approving various taxation measures, the means of carrying out the work of the government;

c) To scrutinise the government's general management of the country's affairs. both internal and external; with a view to ensuring that they are properly and efficiently managed.

Therefore by looking at parliament's performance of those functions during the first year of multi-partism. I can proudly say that the major achievements were the very successful performance of the said functions. As can be seen from the official records of parliamentary proceedings, known as *Hansard*, important laws were passed during the year under review; and so was the government budget for the year 1996/97. Governmental policies and activities came under constant scrutiny by way of numerous parliamentary questions which were addressed to, and answered by, the ministers; and certain important treaties or agreements which had been entered to by the government, were given consideration and eventually ratified by Parliament. These are parliament's major achievements, namely the successful performance of all its functions.

Q. 2 What have been its major failures and what should be done to avoid them?

ANS. I can think of no major failures, and I am sure there were none.

Q. 3 Are there any special challenges in leading a multi-party parliament which are distinct from leading a single party one?

ANS. The speaker's responsibility is very much like that of a referee. He/she administers the rules of the game, and no more. In my particular case, when I was speaker of a single party parliament, I was administering the rules which were operational at that time. I am now speaker of a multi-party parliament and I am administering the rules which are operational now. There is no difference in the challenges involved, the main one being the challenge of *impartiality*. Experience from other parliaments around the world shows clearly that a good speaker is the one who applies the rules of the House impartially. It is of course true that in our single-party parliament of yester-years, there were no opposing political parties; but it is also true that there were opposing *interest groups* which were quite visible in the last parliament of the one-party state. Therefore in the application of rules of the House in such circumstance, the speaker was also obliged to ensure that "the minority had their *say*, while the majority had their *way*." The same challenge of ensuring that "the minority have their *say* and the majority have their *way*," is applicable in guiding the deliberations of the new multi-party parliament.

).4 You have been quoted in sections of the media as saying that a number of changes have been made in the parliamentary regulations to make the House more effective in conducting its business. Can you highlight the main changes and why they were made?

NS. The changes are too numerous to enumerate in an answer to a single question like this one. In this specific matter of changing the parliamentary rules in order to accommodate multi-partism in parliament. I would refer any interested person to Chapter One of my recent book entitled *"Essays on the Transition to Multi-Partism in Tanzania,"* published by Dar es Salaam University Press, specifically the section entitled ..." Parliament Amends its Own Rules." page 5.

).5 There have been calls from not only the opposition but also the ruling party as well as the general public that there is need for a constitutional conference to make our constitution more democratic and congruent with the multi-party era we live in. What is your response to such calls?

NS. My own personal response is clearly stated in my book entitled *"Essays on the Transition to Multi-Partism in Tanzania,* Chapter Ten. specifically the section entitled "The Need for a New Mutli-Party Constitution of Tanzania." page 108.

).6 Do you support the call for having private candidates in our electoral system?

NS. My own personal views on the question of private candidates in our electoral system are fully expressed in chapter six of my book entitled *"Essays on the transition to Multi-Partism in Tanzania."* That whole chapter deals only with the specific question of the independent candidate in multi-party elections. pp. 67-75.

).7 Are you happy with the performance of the opposition in parliament during the past one year. Is there any way in which its effectiveness could be improve?

ANS. In order to correctly assess the performance of the opposition in parliament, it is essential first to have a clear understanding of the role of the *opposition in parliament*. It is only thereafter that one can make an assessment as to whether or not the opposition has successfully carried out its proper responsibilities.

The functions of the opposition are outlined in Chapter Nine of my book entitled *"Essays on the Transition to Multi-Partism in Tanzania,"* where the modern functions of parliamentary opposition are listed from page 92 onwards. Therefore my answer to your question is that judging the opposition by their performance of those functions, I can say that they have done very well indeed.

In their first year of existence, their effectiveness will no doubt improve as they gain more and more experience of parliamentary business in the coming years.

Q. 8 It is claimed that the present practice of appointing ministers from among MPs is bad because it waters down their representative role as they are then supposed to support all government proposals which need not be popular with the people. It is therefore proposed that this practice be changed so that ministers should be distinct from members of parliament. What is your opinion on this proposal?

ANS. It should be understood that there are two major systems of government in the world. These are:
a)   The Parliamentary System of Government:
b)   The Presidential System of Government.

The system which is being operated here in Tanzania is the parliamentary system of government, whereby all the ministers must be selected from among the members of parliament, and must be accountable to parliament for the performance of their duties and responsibilities.

Therefore those who claim that the present practice of appointing ministers from among the MPs is bad, are infact arguing for a complete change of system, from the present one of parliamentary government to that of presidential government, whereby the President appoints his ministers from outside parliament, and they become accountable to him alone. From the point of view of accountability, I personally prefer the present system of appointing ministers only from among the members of parliament, for in that way, ministers are not only accountable to parliament, but they can also in addition exercise their representative role in their respective ministries. In other words, because they are the elected representatives of the people, they will be bound to consider the peoples' interest in whatever they do in their ministries, which obviously is a good thing. Because then both the back-bench members of parliament and the government Ministers are equally accountable to the voters who elected them.

If, however, the ministers were to be appointed from outside the membership of parliament, there will be no real difference between them and the ordinary civil servant; in the sense that both categories will be accountable only to the person who appointed them. Such a situation can easily create a divisive sort of scenario between "us" and "them," i.e. "us" the elected representatives of the people; and "them" the unelected ministers, who presumably do not care about the interests of the people!

Q. 9 There is a feeling among the public that the tendency toward block-voting by CCM MPs is threatening to replace parliamentary supremacy with CCM party supremacy in policy making in parliament. This is bad because it obviates any meaningful discussion of issues, it is claimed. Do you agree?

ANS. If there is any such feeling, then it must be based on a misunderstanding of the dynamics of the parliamentary system which is based on electoral competition between various political parties. The truth of the matter is that *any* political party which wins an election, will naturally want to remain in power at least until the end of its five year term.

Being defeated by vote in parliament can be a cause for their removal from power, hence the reason for block-voting, in order to ensure that they are not defeated. I would like to emphasise the fact that this applies to *any* political party which wins a majority in elections. It does not apply to CCM alone, nor is it applicable to

Tanzania alone. It is applicable in all parliamentary systems of government all over the world, for it is based on the well-known principle, that in all parliamentary proceedings, "the minority must have their say, but the majority must have their way." Block-voting is a method of ensuring that the majority will have their way. The assertion that "it obviates meaningful discussion" is entirely wrong, because we are talking of voting, which is the final stage after thorough discussion, of an issue. So during discussion, every member of parliament, as an individual, will have his or her say. But, at the time of voting, the majority party must have its way. That is the accepted principle and the *modus operandi* of the system of parliamentary government. A clear understanding of this will help to clear any remaining uncertainties.

25

PARLIAMENTARY RULES ON LEGISLATIVE BILLS: INTERVIEW WITH *THE DAILY NEWS* - 15TH JANUARY, 1998

Q.1 Am I right to say that legislative bills have to be published for at least 21 days before submission to Parliament?

ANS. Yes, that is correct. This particular requirement is spelled out in Parliamentary Standing Rule No. 67(1)

Q.2 Am I also right to say that the Bunge is scheduled to meet starting February 3, this year?

ANS. That is also correct. February 3rd is the agreed date for commencing the forthcoming Bunge Session.

Q.3 Counting from today, January 15, we have less than 21 days to February 3. We have, only 18 days to go. Am I also right to suggest that as of today no bill has been published as required by the parliamentary rules?

ANS. As far as I am aware, no bill has yet been published as of today, 15th January. Legislative bills must be published in the Official Government Gazette, which is published every Friday by the Government Printer. In order to qualify under the 21 days rule, bills for presentation to Parliament on 3rd February should have been published at the latest by last Friday, 9th January, 1998. But no bills were actually published up to last Friday. It means that any bills which may be published now will have failed to meet the 21 days publication requirement, and they will not be accepted for presentation to Parliament on 3.2.1998.

Q.4 Incidentally how many times has this happened?

ANS. I am not aware of any previous failing in this regard. I believe this is the first time ever that this has happened, and will presumably also be the last!

Q.5 Suppose the Bunge met without legislative bills would that be a violation of any of your rules?

ANS. There would be no violation of the parliamentary rules, because even if there are no bills, Parliament can still deal with other matters. But it is true that apart from the annual budget business, enacting legislation is by far the most important Parliamentary activity. Hence the absence of bills at the February session would make it largely unproductive, and really not even worth the expenditure of convening it.

Q.6 I take non-publication of the legislative bills as a problem, do you have possible solutions to this problem, say pushing the commencement date from February 3 to some other date?

ANS. Yes, there are certain specific solutions to this problem, which are also provided for in our parliamentary rules. One such solution is to ask the President of the United Republic to issue a "certificate of urgency." This is a document which must be signed personally by the President himself, signifying that the said bills are of such an urgent nature that they cannot wait to satisfy the 21 days publication rule. The other possible solution is to postpone the commencement of the relevant session to a later date, in order to give the government more time to complete its bills. This latter solution was recently adopted by the British House of Commons in London, which postponed its return from its summer recess by two weeks, in order to give the government more time to prepare its bills. I personally prefer this second solution, for it also gives more time to MPs to digest the bills before actual discussion takes place inside Parliament.

Q.7 Has this been an over-sight or is it because of something that can be easily explained and understood?

ANS. I have no idea. Government bills are normally prepared by the Chief Parliamentary Draftsman, on specific instructions from the Cabinet. I am therefore not in a position to know who is to blame in this particular case, the Cabinet or the Chief Parliamentary Draftsman. It should be noted that the Chief Parliamentary Draftsman is not an official of Parliament. He is a Government Civil Servant located in the Attorney General's Chambers. So if there is any explanation to be given to Parliament regarding this episode, the responsibility for doing so will be that of the Government itself, and certainly not the Speaker!

www.ingramcontent.com/pod-product-compliance
Lightning Source LLC
Chambersburg PA
CBHW071130280326
41935CB00010B/1170